AP MACROECONOMICS REVIEW

400 PRACTICE QUESTIONS AND ANSWER EXPLANATIONS

Michael Graziosi

All Inquiries should be addressed to:
Island Prep Publishing, Inc.
P.O. Box 1021
Bellmore, NY 11710
info@longislandregentsprep.com

ISBN: 978-1537377766

CONTENTS

Answers 169

ABOUT THE AUTHOR

Michael Graziosi teaches social studies at John F. Kennedy High School in Bellmore, New York. Since 2005, he has taught many courses, including AP Macroeconomics, Economics Concepts, U.S. History, and Criminology. Michael received his undergraduate degree in history Villanova University, and his M.A. in social studies education from Hofstra University. He is also co-founder and co-owner of Long Island Regents Prep, which offers NY State Regents, AP, and SAT review classes in Farmingdale, New York.

INTRODUCTION

Advanced Placement Macroeconomics

Once dubbed the "dismal science", economics has experienced a surge of popularity in recent years. Non-fiction books by authors Michael Lewis, Malcolm Gladwell, Stephen Dubner, and Steven Levitt are regularly found at the top of best-seller lists. Also, the economic crisis of 2008 returned economics to the forefront of the global conversation, particularly macroeconomic concepts about policies used to address urgent economic problems. Perhaps reflecting this popularity, enrollment in AP Macroeconomics has also grown.

While AP Macroeconomics has become more popular, student participation in the greater Advanced Placement program has increased in every subject across every demographic. Simply put, students are taking more AP exams in an effort to prepare for and gain admission to selective colleges. This book is designed to help relieve some of the pressure associated these high-stakes courses, and to provide students with the essential strategies, skills, and content to excel on the AP Macroeconomics exam.

The AP Macroeconomics curriculum includes the most essential concepts of this field of study. The course begins by familiarizing students with the general concepts of economic thought, and then introduces students to the "big picture" perspective of macroeconomics. After learning to understand gross domestic product, unemployment, inflation, and other broad measures of macroeconomic performance, students learn how to determine states of equilibrium, recession, and inflation in the short-run and the long-run. Students then consider the various government actions that can address macroeconomic problems, such as fiscal and monetary policy, and how the mechanics of these policies are conducted in the financial system and the government budgetary process. The course is rounded out with a study of economic growth and the international sector.

AP Macroeconomics requires students to develop their skills in analyzing quantatative data, using objective observation, and logically understanding cause and effect. Students must also master drawing and manipulating several graphs that visually describe important concepts. The questions in this book are organized by topic and difficulty level, and the answer explanations can help guide students through a logical manner of thinking about economic concepts.

The AP Macroeconomics exam consists of a 70-minute multiple-choice section with 60 questions and a 60-minute free-response section. There are three free-response questions that require students to provide written responses, perform calculations, and/or properly labeled graphs. This book contains over 400 questions with detailed explanations to help students review the essential concepts, methods, graphs, and skills to master the AP Macroeconomics exam.

QUESTIONS

Basic Economic Concepts

SCARCITY, CHOICE, AND OPPORTUNITY COSTS

DIFFICULTY LEVEL 1

1. The problem of "scarcity" exists in economics because:
    (A) people have limited needs
    (B) people have limited wants
    (C) all markets have shortages
    (D) there are limited resources to fulfill unlimited wants
    (E) there are unlimited resources and limited demand

2. The basic economic problem of all countries is the existence of
    (A) shortages of goods and services during recessions
    (B) unlimited wants and scarce resources
    (C) wage increases and high production costs
    (D) unemployment and inflation
    (E) rising budget deficits

3. The critical problem of economics is:
    (A) creating laws to protect resources from overuse
    (B) allocating scarce resources to satisfy wants
    (C) providing citizens with welfare and social services
    (D) developing a monetary system
    (E) establishing a system of fair taxation

4. When one decision is made, there are alternatives that are not chosen. The next best alternative not selected is called

   (A) opportunity cost
   (B) scarcity
   (C) comparative advantage
   (D) absolute disadvantage
   (E) production possibility

5. Jiang prefers bicycling to running and he prefers running to swimming. If these are his only three choices, what is his opportunity cost of bicycling?

   (A) bicycling
   (B) running and swimming
   (C) running
   (D) swimming
   (E) the price of the bicycle

6. Which of the following is an example of a resource?

   I.   wheat
   II. an oven
   III. a pizza

   (A) I only
   (B) II only
   (C) III only
   (D) I and II only
   (E) I, II, and III

7. A truck driver recieves safety training. What kind of resource has the truck driver acquired?

   (A) labor
   (B) human capital
   (C) physical capital
   (D) entrepreneurship
   (E) land

DIFFICULTY LEVEL 2

8. Which of the following situations represent scarcity?

   I.   Air pollution in a growing economy.
   II. Floppy disks are no longer being produced.
   III. There is a finite amount of coal in the physical environment.

   (A) I only
   (B) II only
   (C) III only
   (D) I and III only
   (E) I, II, and III

9. Microsoft finds it difficult to hire enough skilled computer programmers. This statement represents the concept of:

   (A) scarce resources are not that costly
   (B) resources are scarce
   (C) unlimited supply of resources
   (D) fixed prices of labor
   (E) physical capital

10. The school cafeteria has pizza, chicken, or cheeseburgers for lunch. You decide to have chicken but if they were out of chicken you would have chosen pizza. The opportunity cost of choosing chicken is:

(A) pizza
(B) chicken
(C) a cheeseburger
(D) pizza and a cheeseburger
(E) pizza, chicken, and a cheeseburger

11. If the supply of all resources were unlimited then:

(A) needs and wants would be limited
(B) technological research would no longer be necessary
(C) goods and services would be distributed equally
(D) the concept of opportunity cost would no longer be relevant
(E) nominal wages would decrease

PRODUCTION POSSIBILITIES CURVE

DIFFICULTY LEVEL 1

1. Suppose the nation of Econoland decides to produce only books and records. According to the production possibilities curve, as book production increases, the production of records will:

   (A) not change
   (B) increase
   (C) increase at an increasing rate
   (D) increase at a decreasing rate
   (E) decrease

DIFFICULTY LEVEL 2

2. What conditions exist if an economy is producing a level of output that is on its production possibilities curve?

   (A) idle resources
   (B) equitable distribution of goods and services
   (C) inefficient use of resources
   (D) no idle resources and efficient use of resources
   (E) inflation and high unemployment

3. A point inside the production possibilities curve represents:

   (A) efficient production
   (B) inefficient production
   (C) an increase in production possibilities
   (D) economic growth
   (E) inflation

4. The production possibilities curve will shift outward for which of the following reasons?

I.   The unemployment rate decreases.

II.   There is a significant natural disaster.

III. A new technology improves worker productivity.

(A) I only

(B) II only

(C) III only

(D) I and III only

(E) I, II, and III

The following three questions refer to the following graph of a country's production possibilities curve.

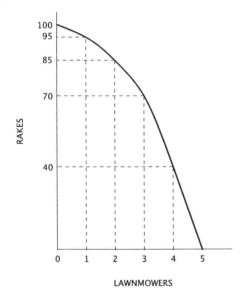

5. If one lawnmower is currently being produced, the opportunity cost of producing the second lawnmower is:

   (A) 100 rakes

   (B) 95 rakes

   (C) 85 rakes

   (D) 15 rakes

   (E) 10 rakes

6. Which of the following combinations of rakes and lawnmowers represents an inefficient level of production?

   (A) 100 rakes and 5 lawnmowers

   (B) 95 rakes and 1 lawnmower

   (C) 85 rakes and 2 lawnmowers

   (D) 70 rakes and 2 lawnmowers

   (E) 40 rakes and 4 lawnmowers

7. The best combination of rakes and lawnmowers for this economy to produce is

   (A) 100 rakes and 0 lawnmowers

   (B) 0 rakes and 5 lawnmowers

   (C) 70 rakes and 3 lawnmowers

   (D) 40 rakes and 4 lawnmowers

   (E) indeterminate with the available information

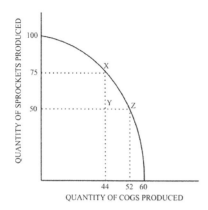

8. On the basis of the diagram above showing an economy's production possibilities curve for two goods, which of the following statements is true?

I. The opportunity cost of moving from point X to point Z is 25 sprockets.
II. The opportunity cost of moving from point Z to point X is 8 cogs.
III. The opportunity cost of moving from point Y to point X is 0 cogs.

(A) I only
(B) II only
(C) I and II only
(D) II and III only
(E) I, II, and III

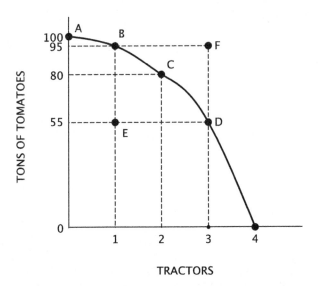

9. On the basis of the diagram above showing an economy's production possibilities curve for two goods, what does Point F represent?

   (A) A level of production that is efficient.
   (B) The best level of production.
   (C) A level of production that is attainable, but not efficient
   (D) A level of production that is unattainable with current resources
   (E) A level of production that can be attained by producing fewer tractors

10. On the basis of the diagram above showing an economy's production possibilities curve for two goods, what does Point E represent?

   (A) A level of production that is efficient
   (B) The best level of production
   (C) A level of production that is attainable, but not efficient
   (D) A level of production that is untattainable with current resources
   (E) A level of production that can only be attained with economic growth

11. Based on the diagram above, suppose the economy is now producing two tractors. What is the opportunity cost of producing a third tractor?

(A) 5 tons of tomatoes
(B) 15 tons of tomatoes
(C) 25 tons of tomatoes
(D) 55 tons of tomatoes
(E) 80 tons of tomatoes

DIFFICULTY LEVEL 3

12. An economy can be using resources more efficiently when:

(A) it can increase its opportunity costs
(B) it can distribute goods and services equitably
(C) it can reduce poverty
(D) it can make industrial production more profitable
(E) it can make some people better off without making others worse off

COMPARATIVE ADVANTAGE, ABSOLUTE ADVANTAGE, SPECIALIZATION AND EXCHANGE

DIFFICULTY LEVEL 1

1. An economy is said to have an absolute advantage in the production of a good if it can:

    (A) produce that good at a lower opportunity cost than another economy

    (B) produce that good at a higher opportunity cost than another economy

    (C) produce that good at an equal opportunity cost than another economy

    (D) produce a higher quantity of that good than another economy

    (E) produce a lower quantity of that good than another economy

DIFFICULTY LEVEL 2

2. An economy is said to have a comparative advantage in the production of a good if it can:

    (A) produce that good at a lower opportunity cost than another economy

    (B) produce that good at a higher opportunity cost than another economy

    (C) produce that good at an equal opportunity cost than another economy

    (D) produce a higher quantity of that good than another economy

    (E) produce a lower quantity of that good than another economy

Use the table below to answer the following questions.

	Cell Phones	Televisions
Northland	40	20
Southland	10	10

3. What is the domestic opportunity cost of producing 1 cell phone in Northland and Southland, before specialization and trade?

	Northland	Southland
(A)	0.5 televisions	1 television
(B)	1 television	1.5 televisions
(C)	0.5 televisions	0.5 televisions
(D)	2 televisions	1 television
(E)	1.5 televisions	2 televisions

4. What is the domestic opportunity cost of producing 1 television in Northland and Southland, before specialization and trade?

	Northland	Southland
(A)	0.5 cell phones	1 cell phone
(B)	1 cell phone	1.5 cell phones
(C)	2 cell phones	0.5 cell phones
(D)	2 cell phones	1 cell phone
(E)	1.5 cell phones	2 cell phones

Use the graph below to answer the following questions.

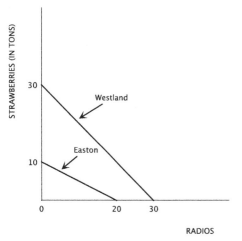

5. What is the domestic opportunity cost of producing 1 strawberry in Easton and Westland, before specialization and trade?

	Easton	Westland
(A)	0.5 radios	1 radio
(B)	2 radios	1 radio
(C)	0.5 radios	0.5 radios
(D)	1 radios	1 radio
(E)	1.5 radios	2 radio

6. According to the diagram, which of the following statements is true?

(A) Easton has an absolute advantage in radio production, Westland has an absolute advantage in strawberry production.

(B) Westland has an absolute advantage in the production of both goods, Easton has a comparative advantage in strawberry production.

(C) Westland has an absolute advantage in the production of both goods, Easton has a comparative advantage in radio production.

(D) Westland has an absolute advantage in the production of both goods, Easton has a comparative advantage in the production of both goods.

(E) Neither country can benefit from trade

7. Under what terms of trade would both Easton and Westland find it mutually beneficial to specialize and trade?

(A) 1 ton of strawberries = 3 radios

(B) 1 ton of strawberries = 1.5 radios

(C) 1 ton of strawberries = 1 radio

(D) 1 ton of strawberries = 0.5 radios

(E) There are no terms of trade that would enable both countries to benefit because Westland has an absolute advantage in both goods

The following questions are based on the table below, which indicates labor-hours needed to produce a single unit of each of two goods in each of two nations.

	Lobster	Bananas
Nation A	10 labor-hours	20 labor-hours
Nation B	15 labor-hours	45 labor-hours

8. If labor is the only factor used to produce the goods, in each nation, what is the opportunity cost of producing one unit of lobster?

	Nation A	Nation B
(A)	0.5 bananas	0.33 bananas
(B)	1 banana	0.5 bananas
(C)	0.5 bananas	3 bananas
(D)	1 banana	1.5 bananas
(E)	2 bananas	3 bananas

9. The table above indicates labor-hours needed to produce a single unit of each of two goods in each of two nations. If labor is the only factor used to produce the goods, which of the following statements must be correct?

I.   Nation A has an absolute advantage in the production of both goods, but a comparative advantage in the production of bananas.
II. Nation B has an absolute advantage in the production of both goods, but a comparative advantage in the production of lobster.
III. Mutually advantageous trade can occur between the two nations when 2.5 units of lobster are exchanged for 1 unit of bananas.

(A) I only
(B) II only
(C) III only
(D) I and III only
(E) II and III only

Basic Economic Concepts

10. If Northland and Southland were to specialize and trade, Northland would find it advantageous to:

(A) export televisions and import cell phones

(B) export cell phones and import televisions

(C) export both cellphones and televisions and import nothing

(D) import both cellphones and televisions and export nothing

(E) trade 3 cell phones for 1 television

DEMAND, SUPPLY, AND MARKET EQUILIBRIUM

DIFFICULTY LEVEL 2

1. The law of demand is illustrated when:
    (A) higher natural gas prices cause gas companies to drill for new sources of natural gas
    (B) an increase in price encourages more people to purchase an automobile because the quality of automobiles has risen
    (C) an increase in the purchases of cell phones results from lower prices
    (D) changing tastes cause more people to purchase diet cola
    (E) lower oil prices cause oil companies to drill fewer oil wells

2. If people demand more honey when the price of tea falls, then honey and tea are:
    (A) substitutes
    (B) complements
    (C) normal goods
    (D) capital goods
    (E) not related

3. Suppose yams and sweet potatoes are considered to be substitutes. Holding everything else constant, if the price of yams increases, then
    (A) demand for sweet potatoes will increase
    (B) demand for sweet potatoes will decrease
    (C) demand for yams will increase
    (D) demand for yams will decrease
    (E) demand for both yams and sweet potatoes will decrease

4. If technological advance occurs that makes the production of cell phones more efficient, which of the following statements is true?

    (A) The demand for cell phones will increase.

    (B) The supply of cell phones will increase.

    (C) The demand for cell phones will decrease.

    (D) The supply of cell phones will increase.

    (E) There will be no change in the demand or supply of cell phones.

5. A shift to the left of a supply curve is caused by

    (A) an increase in worker productivity

    (B) an increase in consumers' income

    (C) a increase in the cost of a productive input

    (D) a decrease in the price of a substitute good

    (E) an advancement in technology needed to produce the good

The following question refers to the diagram below, which shows the demand and supply of sandwiches per week.

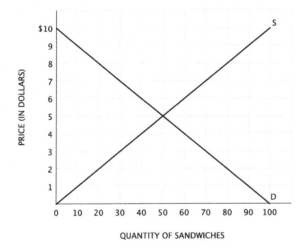

QUANTITY OF SANDWICHES

6. At a market price of $7, which of the following conditions will occur?

    (A) Shortage of 40 sandwiches
    (B) Shortage of 20 sandwiches
    (C) Market equilibrium
    (D) Surplus of 20 sandwiches
    (E) Surplus of 40 sandwiches

7. Suppose the population in an economy were to increase. Which of the following would occur?

    I.   Equilibrium price would increase.
    II. Equilibrium quantity would increase
    III. Equilibrium quantity supplied would increase.

    (A) I only.
    (B) II only.
    (C) III only.
    (D) I and II only.
    (E) I, II, and III.

8. Which of the following changes will definitely result in an increase in both the equilibrium price and quantity of a good?

	Supply	Demand
(A)	Increase	Increase
(B)	Increase	No change
(C)	No change	Increase
(D)	Decrease	Increase
(E)	Decrease	Decrease

MACROECONOMIC ISSUES: BUSINESS CYCLE, UNEMPLOYMENT, INFLATION, GROWTH

DIFFICULTY LEVEL 1

1. A recession is best described as:

    (A) a period in which output and employment are rising

    (B) a period in which inflation is rising 50% annually

    (C) a period in which output and price level are rising

    (D) a period in which output and employment do not change

    (E) a period in which output and employment are falling

2. In a typical business cycle, the business cycle peak is followed by the:

    (A) recession

    (B) recovery

    (C) expansion

    (D) trough

    (E) boom

Use the graph below to answer the question that follows.

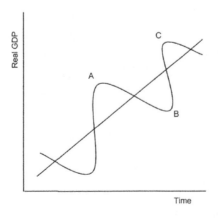

3. In the above diagram of a business cycle, the movement from Point A to B is called:

   (A) a trough
   (B) a contraction
   (C) a peak
   (D) an expansion
   (E) an inflation

DIFFICULTY LEVEL 2

4. The alternation between expansion and contraction in the economy is called the:

   (A) equilibrium cycle
   (B) recession cycle
   (C) commercial cycle
   (D) productivity cycle
   (E) business cycle

5. Economic expansion is typically associated with which trend?

   (A) a decrease in wages
   (B) a falling unemployment rate
   (C) an increase in welfare payments
   (D) a decrease in corporate profits
   (E) a decrease in aggregate output

6. In a command economy, who determines what to produce and how much to produce?

   (A) commercial banks
   (B) markets and the government
   (C) a private planning agency
   (D) a central planning agency
   (E) an international planning agency

Basic Economic Concepts

7. Which of the following problems definitely exists in an economic recession?

   I.   Unemployment
   II.   Inflation
   III. Underutilization of resources

   (A) I only.
   (B) II only.
   (C) III only.
   (D) I and III only.
   (E) I, II, and III.

Measurement of Economic Performance

NATIONAL INCOME ACCOUNTS

TOPIC 1: CIRCULAR FLOW

DIFFICULTY LEVEL 2

1. In a simple circular-flow diagram, households _____ goods and services and _____ factors of production.

    (A) buy; buy
    (B) buy; sell
    (C) sell; sell
    (D) sell; buy
    (E) barter; sell

2. According to the circular flow model, which of the following statements is true?

    (A) Households are demanders in both the factor and product markets.
    (B) Households are demanders in the product markets and suppliers in the factor markets.
    (C) The government is a demander in the product market but not in the factor market.
    (D) Firms are demanders in the product market in suppliers in the factor markets.
    (E) Firms are suppliers in both the factor and product markets.

3. Which of the following is NOT a part of a household's income?

   (A) wages
   (B) savings
   (C) profit
   (D) rent
   (E) interest

Use the diagram below to answer the following questions.

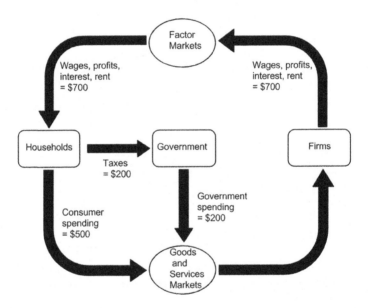

4. According to the circular flow diagram, how does the government fund its spending?

   (A) Consumer spending
   (B) Sales of factor resources
   (C) Profit
   (D) Taxes
   (E) Sales of goods and services

5. According to the circular flow diagram, what is the GDP in this economy?

   (A) $200
   (B) $500
   (C) $700
   (D) $1200
   (E) $1600

6. According to the circular flow diagram, what is the GDP in this economy?

   (A) $725
   (B) $800
   (C) $875
   (D) $900
   (E) $1600

DIFFICULTY LEVEL 3

7. Which of the following economic behaviors is considered to be a leakage from the circular flow model?

   (A) saving
   (B) consumption spending
   (C) investment spending
   (D) government spending
   (E) imports

Use the diagram below to answer the following questions.

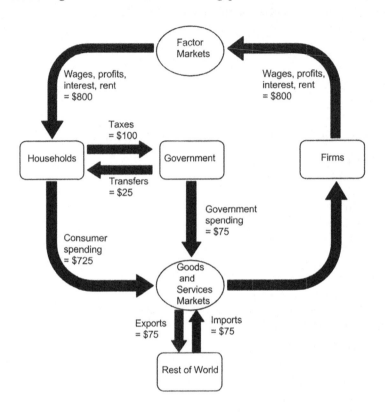

8. According to the circular flow diagram, which of the following statements is true?

   I.   A household's income equals its expenditures.
   II. The government's income equals its expenditures.
   III. Net exports are equal to $75.

   (A) II only
   (B) III only
   (C) I and II only
   (D) I, II, and III

TOPIC 2: GDP

DIFFICULTY LEVEL 1

9. Gross domestic product is defined as

    (A) consumer spending + transfers + government spending + exports – imports
    (B) consumer spending + investment spending + government spending + exports + imports
    (C) consumer spending + investment spending + government spending + exports – imports
    (D) consumer spending + government spending + investment spending + imports – exports
    (E) consumer spending + government spending + financial spending + exports – imports

DIFFICULTY LEVEL 2

Use the table below to answer the following question.

Wages and Salaries	$1000
Profits	$1600
Consumption Spending	$1800
Imports	$200
Exports	$100
Unemployment Benefits	$100
Interest	$400
Government Purchases of Goods and Services	$1100
Sales Taxes	$300
Rent	$200
Investment Spending	$400

10. Using the information in the table above, what is the GDP in this economy?

    (A) $2900
    (B) $3200
    (C) $3300
    (D) $3400
    (E) $4500

11. In an economy with a GDP of $4000, income from wages is $1200, rent is $1100, and interest is $1000. What are profits equal to?

    (A) $700
    (B) $900
    (C) $1000
    (D) $3300
    (E) $4000

Use the table below to answer the following questions.

Personal consumption spending	$600
Domestic investment spending	$300
Imports	$40
Exports	$20
Local government purchases of goods and services	$300
Federal Government purchases of goods and services	$200

12. According to the data in the table above, how much of gross domestic product is the result of government spending?

    (A) $55
    (B) $100
    (C) $200
    (D) $300
    (E) $500

13. According to the data in the table above, what is the value of net exports?

(A) -$40

(B) -$20

(C) $40

(D) $20

(E) $0

14. According to the data in the table above, what is the gross domestic product in this economy?

(A) $600

(B) $1180

(C) $1380

(D) $1420

(E) $1460

DIFFICULTY LEVEL 3

15. A farmer sells cucumbers to a food processor for $1.50 per pound. The food processor makes the cucumbers into pickles and sells each jar of pickles to a grocery store for $2.50. The grocery store sells each jar of pickles for $3.00. How much do these transactions add to GDP?

(A) $1.50

(B) $3.00

(C) $5.50

(D) $7.00

(E) These transactions do not add any value to GDP.

DIFFICULTY LEVEL 2

16. Which of the following examples is classified as consumption spending that would be counted toward the United States' GDP this year?

   (A) The purchase of a computer by an accounting firm.

   (B) The purchase of a computer by a police department.

   (C) The purchase of a computer by a high school student.

   (D) The purchase of a computer produced in the United States by a German student.

   (E) The purchase of a used computer.

17. Which of the following examples is classified as investment spending that would be counted toward this year's GDP?

   (A) Leonard purchased a home built in 1927.

   (B) Hillary purchased a new dishwasher for her apartment.

   (C) Pierre purchased a new luxury car.

   (D) Ace Company purchased 9,000 shares of Microsoft stock.

   (E) Damian purchased a new oven for his restaurant.

18. Which of the following is not considered a part of this year's GDP?

   (A) A family's purchase of a new car.

   (B) A factory's purchase of a new drill press.

   (C) A child's purchase of a school lunch.

   (D) A college student's purchase of a used textbook.

   (E) A government's purchase of a new copy machine.

19. A lawn mower purchased by a private individual is considered to be

    (A) consumption spending
    (B) investment spending
    (C) a purchase of a financial asset
    (D) an import
    (E) human capital

20. Which of the following transactions would cause an increase in a nation's gross domestic product?

    (A) A grandfather sells his house to his grandson.
    (B) An auto dealer sells a car from last year's inventory.
    (C) Mrs. Jones buys a share of stock in a computer company.
    (D) The government purchases new computer equipment for use by public schools.
    (E) Consumers purchase more imported cheese.

21. Which of the following transactions is NOT included in the United States' gross domestic product for the year 2000?

    (A) The rent paid in 2000 by tenants in a house built in 1980.
    (B) The value of an old desk sold by an antique shop.
    (C) The value of a new sofa purchased from a furniture showroom in 2000.
    (D) Commissions earned in 2000 by an auto salesperson.
    (E) The value of automobiles produced in 2000 entirely in the United States by a firm owned by German citizens.

DIFFICULTY LEVEL 3

22. An automobile is produced in 2013, but is not sold until 2014. How is this automobile counted in GDP?

(A) It is included in GDP as consumption spending in 2013.

(B) It is included in GDP as investment spending in 2013.

(C) It is included in GDP as investment spending in 2014.

(D) It is excluded from GDP until it is sold in 2014.

(E) It is excluded from GDP for both 2013 and 2014.

TOPIC 4: REAL VERSUS NOMINAL GROSS DOMESTIC PRODUCT

DIFFICULTY LEVEL 1

23. Real GDP is nominal GDP adjusted for

(A) net exports

(B) real interest rates

(C) inflation

(D) unemployment

(E) government spending

24. Consider an economy that only produces two goods: record players and headphones. If 5 record players are sold at $20 each and 10 sets of headphones are sold at $10 each, then nominal GDP is

(A) $30

(B) $200

(C) $250

(D) $300

(E) $500

Use the table below to answer the following question.

	1999 quantity	1999 price	2000 quantity	2000 price
Record players	5	$20	10	$20
Headphones	10	$10	10	$20

25. According to the data in the table, what is real gross domestic product in 2000, using 1999 as the base year?

(A) $100

(B) $150

(C) $300

(D) $400

(E) $600

DIFFICULTY LEVEL 3

26. If nominal gross domestic product is increasing at 8 percent per year and real gross domestic product is increasing at 4 percent per year, which of the following statements must be true?

(A) The price level is increasing.

(B) Unemployment is increasing.

(C) The economy is experiencing stagflation.

(D) The national debt is increasing.

(E) Exports are increasing.

27. If real GDP for a given year is $1000 and nominal GDP is $1500, then the GDP deflator is

    (A) 67
    (B) 100
    (C) 150
    (D) 200
    (E) 250

28. If the nominal GDP of an an economy increased in 2000 relative to the previous year, it must be true that in this economy in 2000

    (A) the price level has increased and/or the real GDP has increased
    (B) the price level increased by a smaller percentage than the real GDP
    (C) both the price level and the real GDP have increased
    (D) neither the price level nor the real GDP has increased
    (E) the price level increased by a larger percentage than real GDP

INFLATION MEASUREMENT AND ADJUSTMENT

TOPIC 1: PRICE INDICES

DIFFICULTY LEVEL 1

1. What does the consumer price index (CPI) measure?

    (A) The prices of net exports.

    (B) The prices of all goods and services produced in the economy.

    (C) The prices of a specific sample of goods and services purchased by consumers.

    (D) The value of gross domestic product in real dollars.

    (E) The prices of a sample of raw materials purchased by firms.

DIFFICULTY LEVEL 2

2. Suppose that a typical consumer buys the following quantities of three products in 1999 and 2000.

Product	Quantity	1999 Price per unit	2000 Price per unit
Clothing	4 units	$10.00	$11.00
Shelter	2 units	$15.00	$15.00
Food	6 units	$5.00	$6.00

Which of the following can be concluded about the consumer price index (CPI) from 1999 to 2000?

    (A) It decreased by 15%.

    (B) It decreased by 10%.

    (C) It increased by 10%.

    (D) It increased by 15%.

    (E) It remained unchanged.

35

3. The cost of a market basket of goods and services is $200 in Year 1 and $220 in Year 2. If Year 1 is the base year, what is the price index for Year 1?

   (A) 100
   (B) 110
   (C) 115
   (D) 120
   (E) 125

4. The cost of a market basket of goods and services is $200 in Year 1 and $220 in Year 2. If Year 1 is the base year, what is the price index for Year 2?

   (A) 100
   (B) 110
   (C) 115
   (D) 120
   (E) 125

5. The cost of a market basket of goods and services is $180 in Year 1 and $240 in Year 2. If Year 2 is the base year, the price index for Year 1 is

   (A) 75
   (B) 90
   (C) 100
   (D) 125
   (E) 133

Use the following table to answer the following questions.

The Consumer Price Index	
Year	CPI
1	75
2	100
3	110
4	125
5	150

6. The rate of inflation from Year 2 to Year 3 is

   (A) 10 percent
   (B) 25 percent
   (C) 30 percent
   (D) 50 percent
   (E) 110 percent

7. The rate of inflation from Year 4 to Year 5 is

   (A) 10 percent
   (B) 25 percent
   (C) 50 percent
   (D) 110 percent
   (E) 125 percent

8. If the consumer price index rises from 100 to 200, then which of the following is true?

   (A) all prices of production inputs have doubled
   (B) each person's real income has been cut in half
   (C) all prices in the economy have doubled
   (D) the prices in an average consumer's market basket have doubled
   (E) consumer incomes have doubled

9. If a market basket of goods and services costs $90 in the base year and $135 in the current year, what is the value of the GDP deflator?

   (A) 90
   (B) 100
   (C) 125
   (D) 135
   (E) 150

10. In a particular year, the nominal GDP in Econoland was $100 billion while the real GDP was $80 billion. According to this data, what was the GDP deflator that year?

    (A) 80
    (B) 100
    (C) 125
    (D) 133
    (E) 150

TOPIC 2: NOMINAL AND REAL VALUES

DIFFICULTY LEVEL 2

11. A borrower signed a long-term loan agreement with a fixed nominal interest rate of 4 percent. When the agreement was signed, the inflation rate was expected to be 2 percent. If the actual inflation rate were lower than expected, which of the following would be true?

    (A) The real interest rate would be lower than expected.
    (B) The nominal interest rate would be higher than expected.
    (C) The nominal interest rate would decrease.
    (D) The borrower would benefit.
    (E) The lender would benefit.

12. In the country of Econoland, banks charge 8 percent interest on all loans. If the economy's price level has been increasing at a rate of 3 percent per year, what is the real interest rate in Econoland?

    (A) 11%
    (B) 8%
    (C) 5%
    (D) 3%
    (E) 2%

13. If the actual rate of inflation were less than the expected rate of inflation, which of the following would be true?

(A) The real interest rate would remain unchanged.

(B) People who borrowed funds at the nominal interest rate during this time period would lose.

(C) Banks that provided fixed rate loans at the nominal interest rate during this time period would lose.

(D) Unemployment would decrease due to increased investment and spending.

(E) Inflation had been underpredicted.

14. A bank is currently issuing auto loans at an interest rate of 7%. If expected inflation is 3%, then which of the following is true?

(A) The real interest rate is 7% and the nominal interest rate is 3%.

(B) The bank will benefit if the inflation rate unexpectedly rises to 5%.

(C) The real interest rate would increase if the bank decided to issue the loan at 6%.

(D) The real interest rate is 4% and the nominal interest rate is 7%.

(E) The real interest rate is 7% and the nominal interest rate is 4%.

15. If an economy has experienced unanticipated inflation, which of the following groups has most likely benefitted?

(A) Retired workers who have fixed incomes.

(B) Banks that have issued loans at a fixed interest rate.

(C) Homeowners who have fixed-rate mortgages.

(D) Business owners who earn high incomes.

(E) Borrowers who have variable-rate loans.

16. Rafael plans to take out a 3-year loan to purchase furniture. The annual inflation rate is expected to be 6 percent over the next 3 years. If Rafael decides not to take out the loan if the real interest rate exceeds 4 percent, the highest nominal interest rate he is willing to pay is

(A) 4 percent

(B) 5 percent

(C) 10 percent

(D) 15 percent

(E) 25 percent

TOPIC 3: COSTS OF INFLATION

DIFFICULTY LEVEL 2

17. Due to inflation, Shirley must visit he bank frequently to reduce her cash holdings. Emily is experiencing a

(A) menu cost

(B) shoe-leather cost

(C) unit of account cost

(D) store of value cost

(E) search cost

18. As improving technology has made it easier to manage one's money and assets, which of the following inflation costs has been reduced?

(A) shoe-leather costs

(B) menu costs

(C) unit of account costs

(D) search costs

(E) money supply costs

19. Which of the following examples represents the menu costs of rising prices?

   (A) Sean must seek out lower prices when purchasing groceries.
   (B) Robert hires additional staff to update prices at his hardware store.
   (C) Mariel struggles to decide whether $100 is a fair price for a new television.
   (D) Lisa's phone bill now accounts for a larger percentage of her monthly expenses.
   (E) Jean purchases a new car immediately before he expects prices to rise.

20. What are the unit-of-account costs that result from inflation?

   (A) Costs due to the decrease in the purchasing power of money.
   (B) The increased time and effort in using money to make purchases.
   (C) The increased difficulty of using a bank account.
   (D) The loss of reliability in using money to measure the value of goods and services.
   (E) The increase in interest rates resulting from the rising inflation rate.

21. Tonya earned a 5% raise in her wage during the past year. Prices in the economy have increased by 3% during the past year. Given this information, Tonya's real wage has

   (A) increased by 5%.
   (B) increased by 2%.
   (C) remained constant.
   (D) decreased by 2%.
   (E) decreased by 5%.

UNEMPLOYMENT

TOPIC 1: DEFINITION AND MEASUREMENT

DIFFICULTY LEVEL 1

1. The labor force is comprised of
   (A) the total population of an economy
   (B) the total number of people who are employed
   (C) the total number of working age people
   (D) the total number of people who are employed or unemployed
   (E) the total number of people who are unemployed

DIFFICULTY LEVEL 2

2. Which of the following individuals is considered officially unemployed?
   (A) Clarence, a doctor who retired after turning 65 four months ago
   (B) Madison, who resigned from her job at a hardware store to find work as a carpenter
   (C) Julie, who has not worked in 2 years and has given up looking for work
   (D) Frank, who is working part-time and is seeking a full-time job
   (E) Jin, a college student who plans to begin his job search after graduation

3. Which of the following groups is considered officially unemployed?
   (A) People who are discouraged and have given up looking for work
   (B) People who have resigned from their job to start their own business
   (C) People who have quit their job to stay at home and care for children
   (D) People who are seeking to volunteer for charity organizations
   (E) People who were fired from a previous job but are actively seeking a new job

Use the table below to answer the following question.

Labor Market Data for Economy ABC (in millions of persons)

Population	175
Employed	93
Unemployed	7
Not in labor force	75

4. Based on the data in the table above, what is the unemployment rate for Economy ABC?

(A) 3.3%

(B) 4.0%

(C) 7.0%

(D) 8.0%

(E) 10.0%

Use the table below to answer the following question.

Labor Market Data for Atlantis (in millions of persons)

Population	170
Full-time employed	75
Part-time employed	20
Unemployed	5
Discouraged workers	5
Retired workers	33

5. According to the table, what is the unemployment rate in this economy?

(A) 3.0%

(B) 5.0%

(C) 7.5%

(D) 10%

(E) 25%

DIFFICULTY LEVEL 3

6. The actual unemployment level of an economy may be understated by the official unemployment rate because

(A) all unemployed teenagers are not counted.

(B) discouraged workers are counted as employed.

(C) frictionally unemployed workers are counted as unemployed.

(D) underemployed workers are counted as employed.

(E) retired workers are not counted.

TOPIC 2: TYPES OF UNEMPLOYMENT

DIFFICULTY LEVEL 1

7. When workers lose their jobs because of a recession, what type of unemployment increases?

(A) cyclical

(B) structural

(C) seasonal

(D) frictional

(E) foreign

8. Many websites allow job seekers to apply for jobs, post resumes, and more efficiently communicate with potential employers. If these websites increase in popularity, there will likely be

   (A) an increase in the unemployment rate
   (B) a decrease in the frictional unemployment rate
   (C) a decrease in the labor force participation rate
   (D) an increase in structural and frictional unemployment rates
   (E) a decrease in cyclical, but not in frictional unemployment rates

9. Which of the following situations best exemplifies structural unemployment?

   (A) As the summer season closes, lifeguards at beaches are no longer employed.
   (B) Workers increasingly seek jobs with higher salaries.
   (C) A recession causes layoffs at an auto factory.
   (D) Warehouse workers become unemployed when their employer installs automated computer technology.
   (E) There has been an increase in demand for unskilled workers.

10. Which of the following is an example of structural unemployment?

   (A) A worker who loses his job due to a recession
   (B) A farm worker who is unemployed every winter season
   (C) A recent college graduate who is seeking her first job
   (D) A doctor who quit his job to become a full-time volunteer
   (E) A water meter reader whose job has been replaced by a computerized meter

11. Last week Vanessa quit her job as a graphic designer. She has spent the past few days browsing job listings but has not found a new job that matches her skills. Vanessa is best classified as

    (A) frictionally unemployed
    (B) structurally unemployed
    (C) a discouraged worker
    (D) out of the labor force
    (E) cyclically unemployed

TOPIC 3: NATURAL RATE OF UNEMPLOYMENT

DIFFICULTY LEVEL 2

12. An economy has achieved the natural rate of unemployment when

    (A) there is no cyclical and no frictional unemployment.
    (B) the actual rate of unemployment is zero percent.
    (C) there is no cyclical unemployment.
    (D) there is no structural unemployment.
    (E) the actual rate of unemployment is more than the full employment rate.

13. When the economy is at full employment, what is the actual rate of unemployment equal to?

    (A) the cyclical rate of unemployment
    (B) the structural rate of unemployment
    (C) the seasonal rate of unemployment
    (D) the natural rate of unemployment
    (E) zero percent unemployment

14. What type of unemployment causes the actual rate of unemployment to deviate from the natural rate of unemployment?

(A) seasonal
(B) cyclical
(C) frictional
(D) potential
(E) structural

15. If the actual rate of unemployment is 7.0% and the natural rate of unemployment is 5.0% then which of the following is necessarily true?

(A) The frictional unemployment rate is 2%
(B) The structural unemployment is 1.5%
(C) The cyclical unemployment rate is 2%
(D) The cyclical unemployment rate is 12%
(E) The cyclical unemployment rate and structural unemployment rate are both 2%

DIFFICULTY LEVEL 3

16. Which of the following factors would likely cause an increase in the natural rate of unemployment?

(A) An increase in unemployment benefits
(B) An increase in job training
(C) An increase in employment subsidies
(D) A decrease in the minimum wage
(E) A decrease in cyclical unemployment

National Income and Price Determination

AGGREGATE DEMAND

TOPIC 1: DETERMINANTS OF AGGREGATE DEMAND

DIFFICULTY LEVEL 2

1. All other things unchanged, an increase in the price level causes

    (A) a rightward shift of the aggregate demand curve.

    (B) an increase in the purchasing power of assets.

    (C) an upward movement along the aggregate demand curve.

    (D) a downward movement along the aggregate demand curve.

    (E) a leftward shift of the aggregate demand curve.

2. Inflation causes the price level to rise in the United States. How does this inflation affect households?

    (A) The purchasing power of wealth increases and consumer spending increases.

    (B) The purchasing power of wealth decreases and consumer spending decreases.

    (C) The purchasing power of wealth remains constant and consumer spending remains constant.

    (D) The purchasing power of wealth decreases and consumer spending increases.

    (E) The purchasing power of wealth increases and consumer spending decreases.

3. How will a decrease in price level affect the interest rate and interest-sensitive spending?

	Interest Rate	Interest-senstive spending
(A)	Increases	Increases
(B)	Decreases	Decreases
(C)	Increases	Decreases
(D)	Decreases	Increases
(E)	Decreases	Remains the same

4. Aggregate demand is measured by adding together which of the following?

(A) domestic spending and imports

(B) domestic private consumption and government spending

(C) consumption, investment, government spending, and net exports

(D) savings, business inventories, profits, and net exports

(E) consumption, investment, government spending, and imports

5. Which of the following examples demonstrates a condition in which consumption spending would most likely increase?

(A) Consumers believe their wages will be cut next year

(B) The government encourages consumers to save for retirement

(C) Congress passes an increase in payroll taxes

(D) The price level increases

(E) Changes in the stock market increases consumers' wealth

Use the graph below to answer the following question.

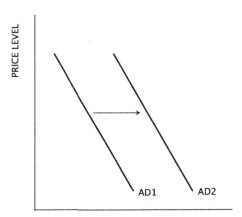

REAL GROSS DOMESTIC PRODUCT

6. Which of the following changes would cause an economy's aggregate demand curve to shift from AD1 to AD2?

(A) An increase in interest rates

(B) An increase in consumer optimism

(C) An increase in spending on imports

(D) A decrease in the money supply

(E) A decrease in the price level in the economy

Use the graph below to answer the following questions.

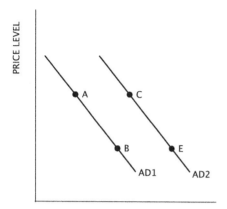

REAL GROSS DOMESTIC PRODUCT

7. A movement from Point A on AD1 to Point C on AD2 can be caused by which of the following changes?

(A) A decrease in overall price level

(B) A decrease in wealth

(C) An increase in interest rates

(D) An increase in overall price level

(E) An increase in government purchases

8. Price level is falling and consumers' wealth and assets increase in purchasing power. Which movement on the graph best represents this change?

(A) From Point E to Point C

(B) From Point E to Point B

(C) From Point C to Point B

(D) From Point A to Point C

(E) From Point A to Point B

DIFFICULTY LEVEL 3

9. A decrease in which of the following would cause the aggregate demand curve to shift to the right?

    (A) Population
    (B) Value of the stock market
    (C) Labor productivity
    (D) Imports
    (E) Consumer optimism

10. When the government runs a budget deficit, it increases its demand of loanable funds, crowding out private investment spending. Which movement on the graph represents the resulting increase in interest rates?

    (A) From Point E to Point C
    (B) From Point E to Point B
    (C) From Point C to Point B
    (D) From Point A to Point C
    (E) From Point A to Point B

TOPIC 2: MULTIPLIER AND CROWDING-OUT EFFECTS

DIFFICULTY LEVEL 2

11. If the marginal propensity to save is 0.9, then the marginal propensity to consume is

    (A) 0.1
    (B) 0.3
    (C) 0.9
    (D) 1.0
    (E) 10.0

12. If the marginal propensity to consume equals 0.8, then the multiplier is

    (A) 2

(B) 3

(C) 5

(D) 8

(E) 10

13. If the marginal propensity to consume increases, which of the following is necessarily true?

(A) The marginal propensity to save decreases

(B) The marginal tax rate increases

(C) The economy is nearing full employment

(D) Consumption is unaffected when income changes

(E) The unemployment rate increases

14. The value of the spending multiplier increases when

(A) the marginal propensity to save decreases

(B) government spending decreases

(C) tax rates are increased

(D) imports increase

(E) exports decrease

15. Terry's marginal propensity to consume is 0.8. Last year he earned $50,000 in disposable income and spent $45,000. If Terry's disposable income this year increased to $60,000, his consumption spending increased by

(A) $4,000

(B) $5,000

(C) $8.000

(D) $9.000

(E) $10,000

16. Suppose that the marginal propensity to consume is equal to 0.8 in a closed economy with only lump-sum taxes. What is the maximum increase in output that can be caused by a $50 billion increase in government spending?

    (A) $40 billion
    (B) $50 billion
    (C) $100 billion
    (D) $250 billion
    (E) $400 billion

17. Which of the following statements about the marginal propensity to consume is true?

    (A) It is always equal to the money multiplier.
    (B) It is equal to the percentage of total income that is spent on consumption.
    (C) It increases as individuals increase their savings.
    (D) It determines the size of the spending multiplier.
    (E) It is always equal to the marginal propensity to save.

DIFFICULTY LEVEL 3

18. Suppose that autonomous consumption is $500 and that the marginal propensity to consume is 0.75. If disposable income increases by $1100, consumption spending will increase by

    (A) $275
    (B) $375
    (C) $495
    (D) $825
    (E) $1100

19. Which of the following changes will have the smallest expansionary effect on aggregate demand in the short run?

   (A) An increase in consumption of $200
   (B) An increase in government spending of $200
   (C) An increase in exports of $200
   (D) A decrease in savings of $200
   (E) A decrease in taxes of $200

20. Assume an economy with lump-sum taxes and no international trade. If the marginal propensity to consume is 0.75, which of the following is true?

   (A) When income increases by $1, investment increases by a maximum of $4.
   (B) When consumption increases by $4, savings increase by a maximum of $1.
   (C) When consumption increases by $4, investment increases by a maximum of $1.
   (D) When investment increases by $1, consumption increases by a maximum of $4.
   (E) When investment increases by $1, income increases by a maximum of $4.

AGGREGATE SUPPLY

TOPIC 1: SHORT-RUN AND LONG-RUN ANALYSES

DIFFICULTY LEVEL 1

1. The aggregate supply curve shows the relationship between the aggregate output supplied and

   (A) aggregate price level
   (B) aggregate money supply
   (C) aggregate unemployment rate
   (D) aggregate imports
   (E) aggregate real interest rate

2. According to the short-run aggregate supply curve, as price level rises in the economy

   (A) worker productivity rises
   (B) the unemployment rate decreases
   (C) aggregate supply increases
   (D) the quantity of aggregate supply increases
   (E) the quantity of aggregate supply decreases

DIFFICULTY LEVEL 2

3. Which of the following statements is true about the "short-run" period in macroeconomic analysis?

   (A) It is equal to one fiscal year
   (B) It is equal to the time needed to end a recession
   (C) It is a period in which wages and input prices are fully flexible
   (D) It is a period in which wages and input prices are fixed
   (E) It is a period in which price level does not change

4. In the long-run, the price of labor is flexible. What is the resulting effect on the aggregate supply curve?

   (A) It becomes horizontal
   (B) It becomes vertical
   (C) It becomes negatively sloped
   (D) It becomes positively sloped
   (E) It does not change

5. Since wages and input prices are fixed, or "sticky," in the short-run, how will producers likely respond to a increase in price level in the economy?

   (A) Producers will increase production of goods and services
   (B) Producers will decrease production of goods and services
   (C) Producers will not change the quantity of goods and services produced
   (D) Producers will lay off workers
   (E) Producers will reduce purchases of physical capital

DIFFICULTY LEVEL 3

6. What is the effect of an increase in price level on the quanity of aggregate output supplied in the short-run and in the long-run?

	Short-run output	Long-run output
(A)	Increase	Increase
(B)	Increase	Remains the same
(C)	Decrease	Remains the same
(D)	Increase	Decrease
(E)	Remains the same	Remains the same

TOPIC 2: STICKY VERSUS FLEXIBLE WAGES AND PRICES

DIFFICULTY LEVEL 1

7. Employers are reluctant to increase nominal wages during an economic expansion and workers are reluctant to accept wage cuts to nominal wages during an economic downturn. Which term best describes wages in this labor market?

(A) Flexible

(B) Real

(C) Potential

(D) Sticky

(E) Variable

DIFFICULTY LEVEL 2

8. Which of the following choices best describes wages in the short-run and in the long-run?

	Short-run	Long-run
(A)	Fixed	Fixed
(B)	Fixed	Flexible
(C)	Flexible	Flexible
(D)	High	Low
(E)	Low	High

TOPIC 3: DETERMINANTS OF AGGREGATE SUPPLY

DIFFICULTY LEVEL 2

9. Which of the following changes will cause an increase in short-run aggregate supply?

   (A) an increase in nominal wages

   (B) an decrease in personal income taxes

   (C) a decrease in labor productivity

   (D) a decrease in commodity prices

   (E) an increase in the aggregate money supply

10. An increase in nominal wages will most likely result in

   (A) an increase in aggregage demand.

   (B) a decrease in aggregate demand.

   (C) a decrease in short-run aggregate supply.

   (D) an increase in short-run aggregate supply.

   (E) a decrease in long-run aggregate supply.

Use the graph below to answer the following questions.

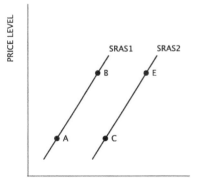

11. A movement from Point A on SRAS1 to Point C on SRAS2 is likely to occur when there is an increase in

    (A) the cost of productive resources

    (B) productivity

    (C) price level

    (D) the federal budget deficit

    (E) the money supply

12. A tax increase of 75 cents per gallon of gasoline would likely cause a movement

    (A) from Point A to Point B

    (B) from Point B to Point A

    (C) from Point B to Point E

    (D) from Point E to Point B

    (E) from Point C to Point B

13. Which movement on the graph would best represent an economy in which a new law is passed mandating a reduction in automobile pollution?

    (A) from Point A to Point B

    (B) from Point B to Point A

    (C) from Point B to Point E

    (D) from Point C to Point B

    (E) from Point C to Point A

14. Which of the following changes will likely cause a movement from Point B on SRAS1 to Point E on SRAS2?

    (A) The shutdown of factories and movement of production of goods abroad

    (B) A decrease in the money supply

    (C) An across-the-board reduction in wages in manufacturing jobs

    (D) An increase in the effective minimum wage

    (E) The passage of a new law requiring improvements in worker safety

15. A movement from Point A on SRAS1 to Point B on SRAS2 is likely to occur when there is an increase in

   (A) the cost of productive resources
   (B) productivity
   (C) price level
   (D) imports
   (E) interest rates

MACROECONOMIC EQUILIBRIUM

TOPIC 1: REAL OUTPUT AND PRICE LEVEL

DIFFICULTY LEVEL 2

1. An increase in government spending will most likely cause the price level and real gross domestic product to change in which of the following ways?

	Price Level	Real Gross Domestic Product
(A)	Increase	Increase
(B)	Increase	Decrease
(C)	Increase	Not change
(D)	Decrease	Increase
(E)	Decrease	Decrease

2. If businesses grow more optimistic and increase their purchases of physical capital, how will the price level and real gross domestic product likely change?

	Price Level	Real Gross Domestic Product
(A)	Increase	Increase
(B)	Increase	Decrease
(C)	Increase	Not change
(D)	Decrease	Increase
(E)	Decrease	Not change

3. An increase in personal income taxes will most likely cause the price level and real gross domestic product to change in which of the following ways?

	Price Level	Real Gross Domestic Product
(A)	Increase	Increase
(B)	Decrease	Decrease
(C)	Increase	Decrease
(D)	Decrease	Increase
(E)	Decrease	Not change

Use the graph below to answer the following question.

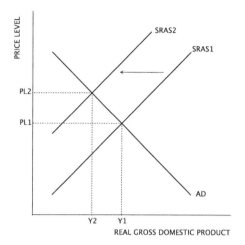

4. Which of the following likely caused the change represented in the graph?

    (A) an increase in the money supply

    (B) an increase in the price of imported oil

    (C) a decrease in the price of imported oil

    (D) an increase in personal income taxes

    (E) a decrease in nominal interest rates

5. If an increase in aggregate supply is followed by a decrease in aggregage demand, which of the following will necessarily occur?

    (A) The price level will increase.

    (B) The price level will decrease.

    (C) Output will increase.

    (D) Output will not change.

    (E) Output will decrease.

6. Stagflation may result from which of the following changes?

   (A) A positive demand shock

   (B) A negative demand shock

   (C) A positive supply shock

   (D) A negative demand shock

   (E) A positive supply shock and a negative demand shock

7. An increase in net exports will likely result in

   (A) increasing aggregate output and a decrease in price level

   (B) a decrease in the unemployment rate

   (C) no change in aggregate output and price level

   (D) a decrease in short-run aggregate supply

   (E) an increase in the price level and unemployment rate

DIFFICULTY LEVEL 3

8. Suppose the aggregate price level is increasing and the equilibrium level of aggregate output is decreasing. An increase in which of the following most likely caused these changes?

   (A) Industrial production

   (B) Government defense spending

   (C) Nominal wages

   (D) The corporate tax rate

   (E) Worker productivity

9. An unanticipated decrease in aggregate output and price level when the economy is in equilibrium will result in

   (A) an increase in unplanned inventories

   (B) an increase in nominal interest rates

   (C) a decrease in unemployment

   (D) a decrease in the money supply

   (E) a decrease in aggregate supply

Use the graph below to answer the following question.

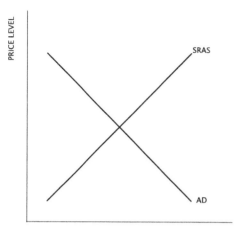

PRICE LEVEL

SRAS

AD

REAL GROSS DOMESTIC PRODUCT

10. According to the graph, which of the following will necessarily result in an increase in output?

I.   A rightward shift of the aggregated demand curve
II. A rightward shift of the short-run aggregate supply curve
III. A leftward shift of the aggregate demand curve
IV. A leftward shift of the short-run aggregate supply curve

(A) I only
(B) II only
(C) I and II only
(D) II and III only
(E) I and IV only

National Income and Price Determination

DIFFICULTY LEVEL 2

Use the graph below to answer the following question.

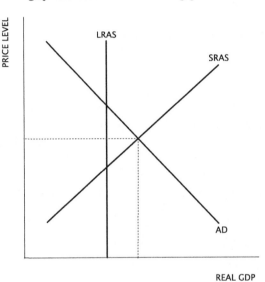

11. According to the graph, which of the following statements about the long-run equilibrium of the economy depicted is true?

(A) The economy will remain in a recession without an expansionary monetary policy.

(B) The short-run aggregate supply curve will shift to the left to restore long-run equilibrium when nominal wages increase.

(C) The economy is in long-run equilibrium.

(D) The unemployment rate will decrease as the economy is restored to long-run equilibrium.

(E) The aggregate demand curve will shift to the left to restore long-run equilibrium.

Use the graph below to answer the following question.

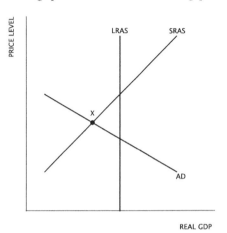

12. If no fiscal or monetary policy is used to address the state of this economy, how will it change in the long-run?

(A) As nominal wages increase aggregate demand will shift to right to restore long-run equilibrium

(B) As nominal wages increase short-run aggregate supply will shift to the right to restore long-run equilibrium

(C) As nominal wages decrease short-run aggregate supply will shift to the right to restore long-run equilibrium

(D) As nominal wages decrease long-run aggregate supply will shift to the left to restore long-run equilibrium

(E) No changes will occur

13. If an economy is currently producing at the full-employment level of output, what will be the effect on the unemployment rate of an increase in the value of the stock market in the short-run and in the long-run?

	Short–run	Long–run
(A)	Increase	No change
(B)	Increase	Increase
(C)	Decrease	Decrease
(D)	Decrease	No change
(E)	Increase	Decrease

Use the graph below to answer the following question.

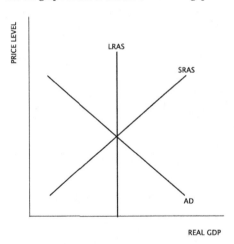

14. In the economy depicted in the graph, what will result in the long-run if the government doubles its spending on health care.

	Output	Price level
(A)	Increase	No change
(B)	No change	Increase
(C)	Decrease	No change
(D)	No change	Decrease
(E)	No change	No change

TOPIC 3: ACTUAL V. FULL EMPLOYMENT OUTPUT

DIFFICULTY LEVEL 2

15. When an economy is in recession, the actual unemployment rate is

(A) equal to the unemployment rate at full employment output
(B) less than the natural rate of unemployment
(C) more than the natural rate of unemployment
(D) equal to the natural rate of unemployment
(E) more than 8 percent

Use the graph below to answer the following question.

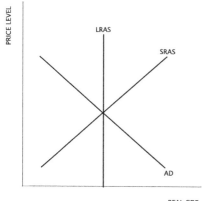

16. According to the graph, which of the following statements about the unemployment rate is true?

(A) Cyclical, frictional, and structural unemployment exist.
(B) The unemployment rate is above the natural rate of unemployment.
(C) The economy is producing above full employment output.
(D) The unemployment rate is equal to the cyclical rate.
(E) The economy is producing at full employment output.

DIFFICULTY LEVEL 2

Use the following graph to answer the question below.

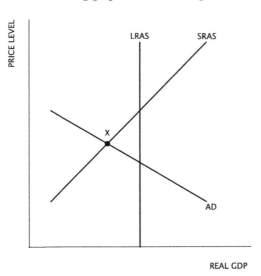

17. According to the graph, if the economy is at point X, there is

(A) long-run equilibrium with full employment.

(B) a recessionary gap with high unemployment.

(C) an inflationary gap with low unemployment.

(D) an inflationary gap with high unemployment.

(E) a recessionary gap with low unemployment.

18. Which of the following statements is true about a recession gap?

(A) The unemployment rate is below the natural rate of unemployment

(B) Aggregate output is below potential output

(C) Potential output is below aggregate output

(D) Aggregate output is above potential output

(E) The economy is experiencing full employment

19. Assuming the economy is in long-run equilibrium, which of the following changes will create an inflation gap?

    I.   An increase in the wealth of households.
    II.   An decrease in the supply of imported oil.
    III. An increase in government spending.

    (A) I only
    (B) II only
    (C) III only
    (D) I and III only
    (E) II and III only

Financial Sector

MONEY, BANKING, AND FINANCIAL MARKETS

TOPIC 1: DEFINITION OF FINANCIAL ASSETS: MONEY, STOCKS, BONDS

DIFFICULTY LEVEL 1

1. Which asset is a share in the ownership of a company held by a shareholder?

   (A) Bond
   (B) Dividend
   (C) Mortgage
   (D) Mortgage-backed security
   (E) Stock

2. What is the benefit when a household purchases a bond?

   (A) The promise of future income
   (B) A share of ownership of a company
   (C) The ability to exchange the bond for goods and services
   (D) Ownership of a piece of property
   (E) Dividend payments from a corporation

3. Which of the following is a financial asset?

   I. A share of ownership in an auto company
   II. An apartment building
   III. A textile factory
   IV. A government bond

   (A) I only
   (B) II only
   (C) I and IV only
   (D) II and III only
   (E) I, II, III, and IV

4. If Eric is using money to purchase gasoline for his car he is using money as

   (A) a unit of account.
   (B) a medium of exchange.
   (C) a transfer of profit
   (D) a store of value
   (E) an interest bearing asset

5. What determines the real value of the United States dollar?

   (A) The quantity of money held as bank reserves
   (B) The money multiplier
   (C) The value of the gold backing the money supply
   (D) The goods and services the dollar will buy
   (E) The interest rate in the loanable funds market

Financial Sector

6. As an economy replaces gold coins with notes that represent gold coins held in reserve, its money supply is evolving from

   (A) fiat money to commodity money
   (B) commodity money to fiat money
   (C) commodity-backed money to fiat money
   (D) commodity-backed money to commodity money
   (E) commodity money to commodity-backed money

TOPIC 2: TIME VALUE OF MONEY (PRESENT AND FUTURE VALUE)

DIFFICULTY LEVEL 2

7. If you loan $100 today, what is the future value of the loan one year from now at an annual interest rate of 8%?

   (A) $92
   (B) $100
   (C) $102
   (D) $108
   (E) $116

DIFFICULTY LEVEL 3

8. If the interest rate is 10%, the present value of $1.10 paid to you one year from now is:

   (A) $0.89
   (B) $0.90
   (C) $1.00
   (D) $1.10
   (E) $1.21

9. If you loan $100 at a 5% annual interest rate, what is the real value of the loan one year from now if the inflation rate is 3%?

(A) $95

(B) $100

(C) $102

(D) $103

(E) $105

TOPIC 3: MEASURES OF MONEY SUPPLY

DIFFICULTY LEVEL 1

10. Which of the following are not counted in the money supply of the United States?

(A) currency

(B) coins

(C) checkable deposits

(D) demand deposits

(E) pure gold coins

11. Which of the following includes only the most liquid assets?

(A) M1 money

(B) M2 money

(C) stocks and bonds

(D) mortgage-backed securities

(E) mutual funds

Financial Sector

12. Which of the following constitutes the largest component of the M1 money supply?

(A) currency

(B) coins

(C) savings deposits

(D) checkable deposits

(E) traveler's checks

13. What is the effect of a withdrawal of $500 from a checking account on the M1 measure of the money supply?

(A) It does not change.

(B) It increases by $500.

(C) It increases by less than $500.

(D) It decreases by $500.

(E) It decreases by less than $500.

14. Nancy transfers $2000 from her savings account to her checking account. What is the effect on the M1 measure and the M2 measure of the money supply?

	M1	M2
(A)	Increases by $2000	Increases by $2000
(B)	Increases by $2000	Decreases by $2000
(C)	Decreases by $2000	No change
(D)	No change	Decreases by $2000
(E)	Increases by $2000	No change

Use the table below to answer the following question.

Assets	
Currency	$25
Traveler's checks	$5
Short time deposits (CDs)	$10
Municipal bonds	$60
Savings deposits	$30
Money market funds	$20
Checkable deposits	$70
Gift cards	$50

15. According to the table, what is the value of M1 and M2?

	M1	M2
(A)	$100	$100
(B)	$100	$160
(C)	$130	$160
(D)	$160	$210
(E)	$160	$220

TOPIC 4: BANKS AND CREATION OF MONEY

DIFFICULTY LEVEL 1

16. What are bank reserves?

(A) Deposits that are held in the form of gold reserves

(B) The sum of all loans a bank makes to borrowers

(C) The value of investments a bank keeps in excess of the value of deposits

(D) The fraction of deposits kept as currency or on deposit at the Federal Reserve

(E) The value of owner's equity in the bank

17. The reserve ratio is the fraction of deposits that banks

    (A) have loaned to borrowers.
    (B) invest in securities.
    (C) hold as reserves.
    (D) are required to loan.
    (E) hold as gold reserves.

DIFFICULTY LEVEL 2

18. If the required reserve ratio is 10% and $200 is deposited into a bank, by how much can that bank increase its loans?

    (A) $10
    (B) $20
    (C) $180
    (D) $190
    (E) $200

19. If the required reserve ratio is 10 percent, what is the maximum change in demand deposits possible in the banking system if Denise deposits $25 into her checking account?

    (A) $10
    (B) $25
    (C) $50
    (D) $250
    (E) $400

20. What action must a bank take to create money?

    (A) Lend excess reserves to customers
    (B) Print currency at the Federal Reserve
    (C) Keep all deposits in reserve
    (D) Use all deposits to purchase stocks and bonds
    (E) Purchase Treasury bills from the government

21. If the reserve requirement is 20 percent, then $50 worth of excess reserves in the banking system can lead to a maximum expansion of the money supply equal to

(A) $20
(B) $50
(C) $100
(D) $250
(E) $500

22. If the public increases its desire to hold money as currency, what will the the effect on the banking system?

(A) Banks would be more able to control interest rates.
(B) Banks would be less able to control interest rates.
(C) Banks would be more able to expand credit.
(D) Banks would be less able to expand credit.
(E) Banks would be more able to increase reserves.

23. A bank with no excess reserves receives a $200 deposit from a new customer. If the required reserve ratio is 20 percent, this bank now has excess reserves equal to

(A) $20
(B) $40
(C) $80
(D) $160
(E) $200

24. A bank with no excess reserves receives a $10,000 cash deposit from a new customer. If the required reserve ratio is 20 percent, what is the maximum amount by which this bank may increase its loans?

(A) $2,000
(B) $8,000
(C) $10,000
(D) $20,000
(E) $40,000

Use the table below to answer the following question.

Assets		Liabilities	
Required reserves:	$15,000	Demand Deposits:	$100,000
Excess reserves:	5,000		
Loans:	80,000		

25. According to the information in the table above, what is the required reserve ratio in this economy?

(A) 5%

(B) 15%

(C) 20%

(D) 80%

(E) 100%

DIFFICULTY LEVEL 3

26. Upon receiving a demand deposit of $1000 a bank's excess reserves increased by $850. The required reserve ratio must be

(A) 5%

(B) 10%

(C) 15%

(D) 85%

(E) 150%

Use the table below to answer the following question.

Assets		Liabilities	
Reserves:	$13,000	Demand Deposits:	$100,000
Securities	75,000		
Loans:	12,000		

27. A bank is facing the conditions given in the table above. If the reserve requirement is 11 percent and the bank does not sell any of its securities, what is the maximum additional amount that this bank can loan?

(A) 0
(B) $1430
(C) $2000
(D) $11,000
(E) $13,000

28. If the reserve requirement is 10 percent but banks voluntarily keep some excess reserves, a $5,000 increase in new reserves will result in

(A) an increase in the money supply of $5,000
(B) an increase in the money supply of $50,000
(C) an increase in the money supply of less than $50,000
(D) a decrease in the money supply of $50,000
(E) a decrease in the money supply of more than $50,000

TOPIC 5: MONEY DEMAND

DIFFICULTY LEVEL 1

29. The opportunity cost of holding money is

(A) the nominal interest rate on less liquid assets
(B) the federal funds rate
(C) the discount rate
(D) the mortgage rate
(E) zero

30. Why does the demand for money increase when national income increases?

    (A) The money supply increases
    (B) The budget deficit decreases
    (C) Interest rates increase
    (D) Spending on goods and services increases
    (E) Imports decrease

31. How does an increase in price level affect the money market?

    (A) Money demand increases
    (B) Money demand decreases
    (C) Money demand does not change
    (D) Money supply decreases
    (E) Money supply increases

32. An increase in the use of cell phones to provide electronic payment in stores will likely result in

    (A) an increase in money demand
    (B) a decrease in the money supply
    (C) an increase in nominal interest rates
    (D) a decrease in money demand
    (E) an increased opportunity cost for holding money

33. Assume that there are no fees to access an ATM. If Congress then decides to impose a $5 tax on each ATM transaction, what will be the likely effect?

    (A) The use of ATMs will increase
    (B) Money demand will decrease
    (C) Sellers will only accept cash as payment
    (D) Price level will increase
    (E) Money demand will increase

34. How will households and firms react to an increase in the nominal interest rate for interest-bearing bank accounts?

(A) The quantity of money demanded will increase
(B) The quantity of money demanded will remain constant
(C) The quantity of money demanded will decrease
(D) The amount of money used for transactions will increase
(E) The opportunity cost of holding money will decrease

TOPIC 6: MONEY MARKET AND THE EQUILIBRIUM NOMINAL INTEREST RATE

DIFFICULTY LEVEL 2

35. If the public decides to increase its holdings of currency, which of the following is most likely to increase?

(A) bank deposits
(B) investment spending
(C) price level
(D) the interest rate
(E) the unemployment rate

36. Which of the following will most likely occur in an economy if the quantity of money demanded is greater than the quantity of money supplied?

(A) The money demand curve will shift to the left
(B) The money demand curve will shift to the right
(C) Interest rates will increase
(D) Interest rates will decrease
(E) Excess reserves will decrease

Use the graph below to answer the following questions.

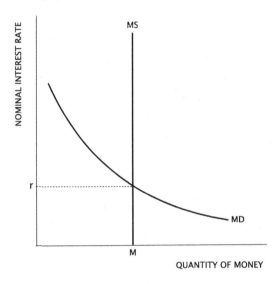

37. According to graph above, what is the likely result if there is an increase in the money supply?

   (A) the nominal interest rate will decrease
   (B) the nominal interest rate will increase
   (C) money demand will increase
   (D) the quantity of money demanded will decrease
   (E) the equilibrium quantity of money will decrease

38. According to the graph, which of the following changes will result in a decrease in the equilibrium nominal interest rate?

   I.   An expansionary monetary policy

   II. An decrease in price level

   III. An increase in real gross domestic product

(A) I only

(B) II only

(C) III only

(D) I and II only

(E) II and III only

LOANABLE FUNDS MARKET

TOPIC 1: SUPPLY OF AND DEMAND FOR LOANABLE FUNDS

DIFFICULTY LEVEL 1

39. What causes firms to demand a higher quantity of loanable funds at a lower real interest rate?

    (A) The government offers subsidies to firms that borrow at lower interest rates
    (B) There is a higher rate of return on investments made at lower interest rates
    (C) There is a lower rate of return on investments made at lower interest rates
    (D) Firms only borrow funds at low interest rates
    (E) Banks cannot loan to firms at high interest rates

40. The loanable funds model demonstrates the interaction of _____ in determining the equilibrium real interest rate.

    Which of the following completes the sentence above?

    (A) households and firms
    (B) government and households
    (C) price level and output
    (D) savers and borrowers
    (E) foreign and domestic consumers

Use the graph below to answer the following questions.

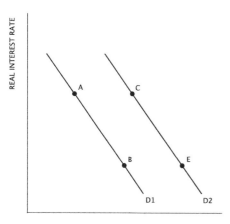

41. Which of the following will most likely produce a movement from Point A on D1 to Point C on D2?

    (A) Corporate profits are expected to decline in the future

    (B) An increase in capital inflows from other nations

    (C) The federal government has a budget surplus

    (D) Households are encouraged to increase their savings

    (E) Firms become more optimistic about future business opportunities

42. A movement from Point E on D2 to Point B on D1 will most likely be the result of

    (A) increased business opportunities after new computer technology is introduced.

    (B) a decrease in government spending that leads to a budget surplus.

    (C) a decrease in taxes that leads to a government budget deficit.

    (D) a decrease in private savings.

    (E) an increase in the marginal propensity to consume.

43. Due to decreased confidence in the financial system, people have increased their savings in foreign financial institutions. What is the likely result on the domestic loanable funds market?

    (A) The demand for loanable funds will increase
    (B) The demand for loanable funds will decrease
    (C) The supply of loanable funds will increase
    (D) The supply of loanable funds will decrease
    (E) The domestic loanable funds market will be unaffected

DIFFICULTY LEVEL 3

44. In the market for loanable funds, the equilibrium interest rate is 4% and the equilibrium quantity of loanable funds is $100 billion. What will be the likely result if financial institutions offer an interest rate of 6%?

    (A) There will be an increase in the quantity of loanable funds demanded.
    (B) There will be an increase in borrowing.
    (C) The quantity of loanable funds supplied will be more than $100 billion.
    (D) The quantity of loanable funds demanded will be greater than the quantity supplied.
    (E) The loanable funds market will remain in equilibrium.

DIFFICULTY LEVEL 2

45. If firms believe that business opportunities will decrease in the future, the demand for loans and the real interest rate in the loanable funds market will likely change in which of the following ways in the short run?

	Demand for Loans	Real Interest Rate
(A)	Decrease	Not change
(B)	Decrease	Increase
(C)	Increase	Increase
(D)	Increase	Decrease
(E)	Decrease	Decrease

Use the diagram below to answer the following questions.

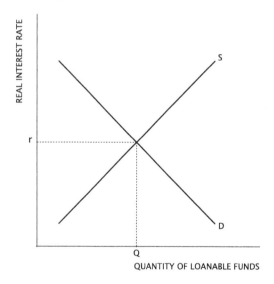

46. According to the graph, an increase in savings by households will

    (A) increase the demand for loanable funds and increase the real interest rate
    (B) decrease the demand for loanable funds and decrease the real interest rate
    (C) increase the supply of loanable funds and decrease the real interest rate
    (D) decrease the supply of loanable funds and increase the real interest rate
    (E) not affect the loanable funds market

47. Which of the following changes will cause an increase in the real interest rate in the loanable funds market?

    (A) The government launches a campaign to encourage the public to increase their savings.
    (B) Firms are optimistic about the housing market and increase construction projects
    (C) The national government reports its second consecutive annual budget surplus
    (D) Foreign savers increase their deposits in domestic financial institutions
    (E) The government increases the money supply

TOPIC 3: CROWDING OUT

DIFFICULTY LEVEL 1

48. Which of the following statements best describes crowding out?

    (A) An increase in the money supply.
    (B) An increase in net exports resulting from a depreciation of the currency.
    (C) An increase in private borrowing subsidized by the government.
    (D) A decrease in private investment resulting from government borrowing.
    (E) An increase in the supply of loanable funds due to increased public and private savings.

49. Government borrowing causes crowding out because

   (A) lower interest rates increase private sector investment
   (B) higher interest rates decrease private sector investment
   (C) higher interest rates increase private sector investment
   (D) a larger money supply increases private sector investment
   (E) a smaller money supply decreases private sector investment

DIFFICULTY LEVEL 2

50. The national government has increased deficit spending on goods and services. In the long-run, which of the following changes would most likely result from this policy?

	Real Interest Rate	Investment
(A)	Decrease	Increase
(B)	Decrease	Decrease
(C)	No change	Increase
(D)	Increase	Decrease
(E)	Increase	No change

51. Which of the following changes will most likely result in crowding out?

   (A) Increase in trade deficit
   (B) Increase in labor productivity
   (C) Decrease in government spending
   (D) Increase in budget deficit
   (E) Decrease in commodity prices

52. Expansionary fiscal policies adopted to counteract a recession tend to result in

   (A) less public spending
   (B) lower prices
   (C) a high rate of economic growth
   (D) higher interest rates
   (E) decreased investment by foreign companies

CENTRAL BANK AND CONTROL OF THE MONEY SUPPLY

TOPIC 1: TOOLS OF CENTRAL BANK POLICY

DIFFICULTY LEVEL 1

1. Which of the following is not a monetary policy tool of the Federal Reserve System?

    (A) setting the reserve requirement
    (B) open market operations
    (C) minting bills and coins
    (D) open market operations
    (E) regulating the banking system

2. The discount rate refers to the price the Federal Reserve System charges for:

    (A) goods and services
    (B) loans to state governments
    (C) loans to banks
    (D) newly printed currency
    (E) U.S. Treasury bills

3. Which of the following best describes the result of a sale of U.S. Treasury bills on the open market by the Federal Reserve?

	Money supply	Interest rates
(A)	Increase	Increase
(B)	Increase	Decrease
(C)	No change	Increase
(D)	Decrease	Decrease
(E)	Decrease	Increase

4. What will likely occur if the Federal Reserve acts to increase the money supply with open market operations?

(A) Bank reserves will decrease.

(B) Bond prices will increase.

(C) The discount rate will increase.

(D) The federal funds rate will increase.

(E) The government budget will move toward surplus

5. Which combination of actions by the Federal Reserve System will cause the greatest increase in the money supply?

	Reserve requirement	Discount rate
(A)	Increase	Increase
(B)	Decrease	No change
(C)	Increase	Decrease
(D)	No change	Decrease
(E)	Decrease	Decrease

6. Which of the following best describes the result of a decrease in the discount rate?

   (A) The demand for money increases and interest rates increase

   (B) The demand for money decreases and interest rates decrease

   (C) The supply of money increases and interest rates decrease

   (D) The supply of money increases and interest rates increase

   (E) Both the demand for money and the supply of money increase and interest rates increase

7. What change in monetary policy can the Federal Reserve enact to reduce the ability of the banking system to create money?

   (A) Decreasing the federal funds rate

   (B) Buying government bonds on the open market

   (C) Decreasing income taxes

   (D) Decreasing the reserve requirement

   (E) Increasing the discount rate

8. Contractionary monetary policy can affect the economy through which of the following chains of events?

   (A) Decreasing government spending lowers the interest rate, which lowers consumption.

   (B) Increasing the discount rate lowers the real interest rate, which raises investment.

   (C) Selling bonds decreases the money supply, which increases the interest rate.

   (D) Increasing taxes increases the reserve requirement, which decreases investment.

   (E) Buying bonds increases the money supply, which lowers the interest rate.

TOPIC 2: QUANTITY THEORY OF MONEY

DIFFICULTY LEVEL 1

9. If nominal gross domestic product in an economy is $1,200 and the money supply is $300, what is the velocity of money?

(A) 3
(B) 4
(C) 12
(D) 40
(E) 300

10. According to the quanity theory of money, if there is a significant increase in the money supply, there will be an increase in

(A) the unemployment rate
(B) the real interest rate
(C) the price level
(D) real output
(E) the velocity of money

DIFFICULTY LEVEL 2

11. If the velocity of money is assumed to be stable in the short-run, the quantity theory of money contends that a decrease in the money supply will lead to a proportional

(A) increase in the unemployment rate
(B) increase in the price level
(C) increase in the nominal interest rate
(D) increase in the real interest rate
(E) decrease in nominal output

TOPIC 3: REAL V. NOMINAL INTEREST RATES

DIFFICULTY LEVEL 1

12. If a lender expects a real interest rate of 5 percent and the inflation rate is expected to be 3 percent, what is the nominal interest rate?

(A) 2 percent

(B) 3 percent

(C) 5 percent

(D) 8 percent

(E) 15 percent

DIFFICULTY LEVEL 2

13. A worker's nominal wage rate has increased from $8 to $10 per hour, while at the same time the general price level has increased by 10 percent. What is the effect on the worker's real wage?

(A) It has decreased by 10 percent

(B) It has decreased by 15 percent

(C) It has increased by 10 percent

(D) It has increased by 15 percent

(E) It has not changed

14. Assume that the nominal interest rate is 8 percent. If the real interest rate is 5 percent, the expected inflation rate is

(A) 3 percent

(B) 4 percent

(C) 5 percent

(D) 8 percent

(E) 13 percent

15. Anna lends $100 to Emily for one year. Anna expects the price level to increase by 8 percent over that year. If Anna wants to maintain the real value of her $100, she should demand payment from Emily of

    (A) $92
    (B) $100
    (C) $108
    (D) $110
    (E) $192

Stabilization Policies

FISCAL AND MONETARY POLICIES

TOPIC 1: DEMAND-SIDE EFFECTS

DIFFICULTY LEVEL 1

1. If the government increases spending on goods and services, it is engaging in

    (A) foreign exchange policy
    (B) fiscal policy
    (C) social policy
    (D) monetary policy
    (E) contractionary policy

2. Which of the following is not a tool of monetary policy?

    (A) Purchasing bonds on the open market
    (B) An increase in the discount rate
    (C) A decrease in personal income taxes
    (D) A decrease in the reserve requirement
    (E) An increase in capital reserve requirements

3. An appropriate fiscal policy to combat inflation would be to increase which of the
    following?

    (A) Military spending
    (B) Sales of government bonds
    (C) The reserve requirement
    (D) Taxes
    (E) Interest rates

4. If the economy is experiencing cyclical unemployment, an increase in which of the
    following will most likely eliminate this type of unemployment?

    (A) Corporate taxes
    (B) Interest rates
    (C) Educational opportunities
    (D) Government spending
    (E) Sales of government bonds

Use the graph below to answer the following questions.

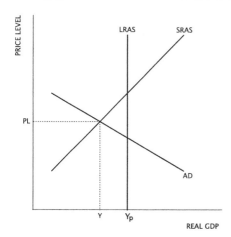

5. Which of the following is an appropriate fiscal policy to return this economy to long-run equilibrium output?

   (A) A decrease in government spending
   (B) A decrease in the discount rate
   (C) An increase in corporate taxes
   (D) A decrease in personal income taxes
   (E) An increase in government bond purchases

6. If the government responds to the economic situation represented in the graph by increasing its purchases of goods and services, what are the likely effects on aggregate demand, price level, and aggregate output?

	Aggregate Demand	Price Level	Aggregate Output
(A)	Increase	Increase	No change
(B)	Increase	Increase	Increase
(C)	Decrease	Increase	Decrease
(D)	Increase	No change	Increase
(E)	Decrease	Decrease	Decrease

7. Which of the following would result if the Federal Reserve lowers the reserve requirement?

   (A) An increase in the budget deficit
   (B) Businesses will increase investment spending on capital goods
   (C) Price level and unemployment will both increase
   (D) The rate of saving will increase
   (E) Net exports will decrease

8. A decrease in taxes and an increase in government spending will most likely change consumption and unemployment in which of the following ways?

	Consumption	Unemployment
(A)	Decrease	Increase
(B)	Decrease	No change
(C)	Increase	Decrease
(D)	Increase	Increase
(E)	No change	Decrease

Use the graph below to answer the following question.

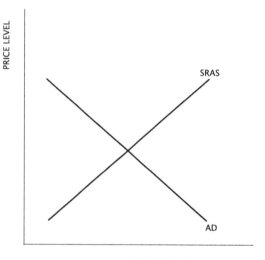

9. According to the graph, which of the following changes will result in a decrease in output?

   I.   An increase in aggregate demand
   II. A decrease in aggregate demand
   III. An increase in short-run aggregate supply
   IV. A decrease in short-run aggregate supply

   (A) I only

   (B) II only

   (C) I and III only

   (D) II and IV only

   (E) II and III only

10. Which of the following changes would reduce an inflationary gap?

    (A) A decrease in the discount rate

    (B) A decrease in the reserve requirement

    (C) A decrease in interest rates

    (D) An increase in government spending

    (E) An increase in the income tax rate

11. A decrease in the money supply will most likely have which of the following effects on real interest rates and real output in the short-run?

	Real Interest Rates	Real Output
(A)	Increase	Decrease
(B)	Increase	Increase
(C)	Decrease	No change
(D)	Decrease	Decrease
(E)	No change	Increase

12. A recessionary gap can be eliminated by all of the following changes EXCEPT

    (A) an increase in government spending

    (B) an increase in net exports

    (C) a decrease in personal income taxes

    (D) a decrease in the interest rates

    (E) a decrease in money supply

13. If exports increase while demand for goods and services produced in other nations decreases, then output, price level, and the unemployment rate will most likely change in which of the following ways?

	Output	Price Level	Unemployment Rate
(A)	Increase	Increase	Decrease
(B)	Increase	Increase	Increase
(C)	Increase	Decrease	Decrease
(D)	Increase	Decrease	Decrease
(E)	Decrease	Decrease	Increase

14. How will a contractionary fiscal policy affect aggregate demand, price level, and output in the short run?

	Aggregate Demand	Price Level	Output
(A)	Increase	Increase	Increase
(B)	Increase	Decrease	Decrease
(C)	Decrease	Decrease	Decrease
(D)	Decrease	Increase	Increase
(E)	No change	No change	No change

15. Which of the following changes would most likely cause the economy to fall into a recession?

    (A) An increase in investment spending

    (B) An increase in the marginal propensity to consume

    (C) A decrease in required reserves

    (D) An open market sale by the Federal Reserve

    (E) An increase in government transfers

16. A increase in purchases of capital stock will most likely result in a decrease in the

    (A) real level of output
    (B) price level
    (C) unemployment rate
    (D) government's budget deficit
    (E) interest rate

17. If the Federal Reserve institutes a policy to reduce inflation, which of the following is most likely to increase?

    (A) Interest rates
    (B) Purchases of U.S. Treasury bills
    (C) Employment
    (D) Government transfers
    (E) Aggregate output

18. How will consumption and real gross domestic product (real GDP) be affected by a decrease in the real interest rate?

	Consumption	Real GDP
(A)	Increase	Increase
(B)	Increase	Decrease
(C)	No change	Increase
(D)	Decrease	Increase
(E)	Decrease	Decrease

19. If the economy of the United States is experiencing a recessionary gap at a very low inflation rate, the Federal Reserve System is most likely to

(A) raise the reserve requirement and sell bonds on the open market to cause an increase in output

(B) lower the discount rate and buy bonds on the open market to cause an increase in output

(C) lower the discount rate and decrease taxes to cause an increase in output

(D) raise the discount rate and lower the reserve requirement to cause an increase in output

(E) pursue an expansionary monetary policy because it is required to do so by law whenever a recessionary gap exists

DIFFICULTY LEVEL 3

20. Which of the following changes will likely result in an increase in aggregate output in the short-run?

(A) An increase in the interest rate

(B) An increase in income taxes

(C) Equal increases in exports and imports

(D) Equal increases in taxes and government spending

(E) Equal decreases in investment and government spending

21. Policymakers want to increase investment in order to reduce unemployment during a recession. Which policy is most appropriate to achieve these results?

(A) An increase in the reserve requirement

(B) A decrease in personal income taxes

(C) An decrease in personal income taxes and an increase in the discount rate

(D) An increase in government spending

(E) An increase in purchases of U.S. Treasury bonds by the Federal Reserve

22. Assume the economy is at full employment and the government wants to increase its spending by $50 billion. How can the government achieve this goal without increasing inflation in the short-run?

(A) Raise taxes by less than $50 billion.

(B) Raise taxes by more than $50 billion.

(C) Raise taxes by exactly $50 billion.

(D) Lower taxes by exactly $50 billion.

(E) Lower taxes by less than $50 billion.

TOPIC 2: SUPPLY-SIDE EFFECTS

DIFFICULTY LEVEL 1

23. Wool is used to produce sweaters, coats, and other types of clothing. If wool prices rise, what will happen to clothing prices and the quantity of clothing sold?

	Price	Quantity sold
(A)	Decrease	Increase
(B)	Decrease	Decrease
(C)	Increase	Increase
(D)	Increase	Decrease
(E)	Increase	No change

24. A decrease in the prices of inputs will cause which of the following changes to occur in the short-run?

	Aggregate Demand	Aggregate Supply	Price Level
(A)	Decrease	No change	Decrease
(B)	No change	Increase	Decrease
(C)	No change	Decrease	Increase
(D)	Increase	No change	Increase
(E)	No change	Increase	Increase

25. Stagflation is caused by

(A) An increase in aggregate demand

(B) A decrease in aggregate demand

(C) An increase in aggregate supply

(D) A decrease in aggregate supply

(E) An increase in the money supply

26. A recessionary gap occurs if

(A) real GDP is equal to potential output

(B) real GDP is greater than potential output

(C) real GDP is less than potential output

(D) the unemployment rate is greater than zero

(E) the unemployment rate is equal to the natural rate of unemployment

27. If the short-run aggregate supply curve intersects the aggregate demand curve to the right of the long-run aggregate supply curve, which of the following is true?

(A) There is a recession gap.

(B) There is an inflationary gap.

(C) Actual output is equal to potential output.

(D) The unemployment rate is greater than the natural rate.

(E) The economy is producing at full-employment output.

28. Which of the following changes would most likely result from an increase in labor productivity?

   (A) An increase in savings and a decrease in interest rates
   (B) A decrease in imports and a decrease in unemployment
   (C) An increase in output and an increase in price level
   (D) An increase in output and a decrease in inflation
   (E) An increase in consumption spending and a decrease in prices

29. Which of the following would most likely result from a contractionary supply shock?

   (A) A decrease in price level
   (B) An increase in aggregate output
   (C) An increase in national income
   (D) An increase in unemployment
   (E) An increase in consumption spending

Use the graph below to answer the following question.

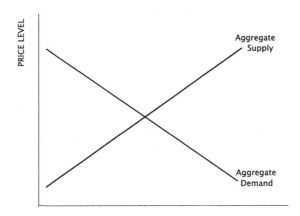

30. According to the graph, how will real gross domestic product and price level be affected by a decrease in the world supply of oil?

	Real GDP	Price Level
(A)	Increase	Increase
(B)	Increase	No change
(C)	Increase	Decrease
(D)	Decrease	Increase
(E)	Decrease	Decrease

31. Assume that firms have grown more efficient and have reduced their energy costs. What is the resulting change in aggregate supply, the price level, and real output?

	Aggregate Supply	Price Level	Real Output
(A)	Decrease	Increase	Increase
(B)	Decrease	Increase	No change
(C)	Increase	Decrease	Decrease
(D)	Increase	Decrease	Increase
(E)	Increase	Increase	Increase

32. A positive supply shock, such as a decrease in fuel prices, will most likely have which of the following short-run effects on output and price level?

	Output	Price Level
(A)	Increase	Increase
(B)	Increase	Decrease
(C)	No effect	No effect
(D)	Decrease	Increase
(E)	Decrease	Decrease

33. An increase in which of the following changes will result in lower inflation and lower unemployment?

    (A) The money supply
    (B) Income taxes
    (C) Energy prices
    (D) Labor productivity
    (E) The minimum wage

34. Suppose that from 1999 to 2000, the unemployment rate increased from 6.8 to 8.1 percent while inflation increased from 2.3 to 5.2 percent. An explanation of these changes might be that the

    (A) aggregate demand curve shifted to the left
    (B) aggregate demand curve shifted to the right
    (C) short-run aggregate supply curve shifted to the left
    (D) short-run aggregate supply curve shifted to the right
    (E) long-run aggregate supply curve shifted to the right

35. Which of the following changes would result in an economy simultaneously experiencing high inflation and high unemployment?

    (A) Inflationary expectations decline
    (B) The labor force participation rate declines
    (C) Government spending increases without increasing taxes
    (D) Factor prices increase due to negative supply shocks
    (E) Labor productivity increases

36. If a decrease in aggregate demand is immediately followed by an increase in aggregate supply, which of the following will necessarily occur?

    (A) The price level will increase.
    (B) The price level will decrease.
    (C) Output will increase.
    (D) Output will decrease.
    (E) Output will not change.

37. Under what conditions would the short-run aggregate supply curve be vertical?

(A) Nominal wages do not change when inflation occurs.

(B) Real wages decrease when inflation occurs.

(C) Nominal wages increase immediately when inflation occurs.

(D) Nominal wages increase slowly when unemployment increases.

(E) Nominal wages adjust slowly to changes in aggregate demand.

38. Assume the economy is currently in a short-run equilibrium at a level of output that is less than full-employment output. If the government takes no policy actions, which of the following changes in price level and output would result in the long-run?

Price Level	Output
(A) Decrease	Decrease
(B) Increase	Decrease
(C) No change	No change
(D) Decrease	Increase
(E) Increase	Increase

39. If aggregate demand increases, how will real gross domestic product and price level change in the long-run?

Real GDP	Price Level
(A) Increase	Decrease
(B) No change	Increase
(C) Decrease	Decrease
(D) Increase	Increase
(E) No change	Decrease

Use the graph below to answer the following question.

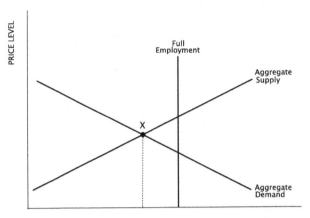

40. The economy in the graph above is currently in equilibrium at Point X. If the government takes no policy action and wages are flexible, which of the following changes will most likely occur in the long run?

(A) Nominal wages will increase and aggregate supply will shift to the right, producing full employment.

(B) Nominal wages will decrease and aggregate supply will shift to the right, producing full employment.

(C) The economy will remain at Point X.

(D) Nominal wages will increase and aggregate demand will shift to the right, producing full employment.

(E) Nominal wages will decrease and aggregate demand will shift to the right, producing full employment.

Use the graph below to answer the following question.

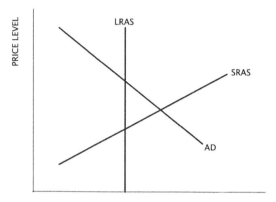

41. If no policy action were taken, which of the following changes would move the economy to its long-run equilibrium?

(A) A decrease in inflation expectations

(B) An increase in wages

(C) A decrease in wages

(D) An increase in investment spending

(E) A decrease in aggregate demand

DIFFICULTY LEVEL 3

42. Assuming the economy is producing at full employment output, a negative supply shock will most likely cause which of the following to the economy in the short-run?

(A) An increase in the price level and a decrease in the nominal wage

(B) An increase in the price level and an increase in the real wage

(C) An increase in the price level and a decrease in the real wage

(D) A decrease in the price level and a decrease in the nominal wage

(E) A decrease in the price level and no change in the nominal wage

Use the graph below to answer the following question.

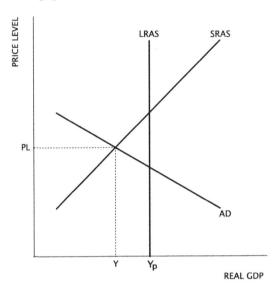

43. According to the graph, how will the economy change in the long-run if no fiscal or monetary action is taken by the government?

(A) Aggregate demand will shift to the right

(B) Aggregate demand will shift to the right

(C) Short-run aggregate supply will shift to the right

(D) Short-run aggregate supply will shift to the left

(E) There will be no change

Use the graph below to answer the following questions.

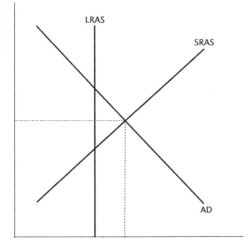

REAL GROSS DOMESTIC PRODUCT

44. Which of the following is true about the long-run equilibrium of the economy depicted in the graph?

   (A) Nominal wages will increase and the short-run aggregate supply curve will shift to the left to restore long-run equilibrium.

   (B) The long-run aggregate supply curve will shift to the right to restore long-run equilibrium.

   (C) An expansionary fiscal policy will restore the economy to long-run equilibrium.

   (D) Aggregate demand will decrease to restore the economy to long-run equilibrium.

   (E) The economy is in long-run equilibrium.

DIFFICULTY LEVEL 2

45. The economy is at full employment and policymakers wish to encourage greater investment while maintaining the price level. Which combination of fiscal and monetary policies would achieve this goal?

	Monetary Policy	Fiscal Policy
(A)	Expansionary	No change
(B)	Contractionary	Expansionary
(C)	Expansionary	Expansionary
(D)	Expansionary	Contractionary
(E)	No change	Expansionary

46. Which of the following combinations of economic policies would be most effective to correct severe inflation?

	Taxes	Money Supply
(A)	Increase	Decrease
(B)	Increase	Increase
(C)	Increase	No change
(D)	Decrease	Increase
(E)	Decrease	Decrease

47. Which of the following includes a combination of fiscal and monetary policies that will bring the economy out of a recession?

(A) Increasing taxes and the discount rate

(B) Decreasing taxes and the money supply

(C) Increasing taxes and the money supply

(D) Increasing government spending and selling government bonds

(E) Increasing government spending and decreasing the discount rate

Stabilization Policies

48. Which of the following changes would comprise the most expansionary fiscal policy?

(A) Increase government spending and the money supply by an equal proportion

(B) Increase payroll taxes and increase government spending by equal amounts

(C) Decrease personal income taxes and government spending by equal amounts

(D) Decrease the discount rate and government spending by an equal proportion

(E) Decrease personal income taxes and increase government spending by equal amounts

49. Assume the government wants to stimulate investment spending in the private sector without increasing the level of real output in the economy. The policy mix that would most likely achieve these results is

(A) an increase in the money supply and a decrease in government spending

(B) an increase in the money supply and a decrease in income taxes

(C) a decrease in the money supply and an increase in government spending

(D) an increase in taxes and a decrease in government spending

(E) a decrease in the money supply and a decrease in income taxes

50. Suppose that the government increases spending and at the same time the central bank conducts a purchase of government bonds. The combined actions will result in

(A) an increase in real gross domestic product and an increase in the interest rate.

(B) an increase in real gross domestic product and an indeterminate change in the interest rate

(C) an increase in real gross domestic product and a decrease in the interest rate

(D) an increase in unemployment and a decrease in the interest rate

(E) an increase in unemployment and an increase in the interest rate

51. If Congress wishes to use fiscal policy to reinforce the Federal Reserve's monetary policy, it should

(A) decrease government spending when the money supply is increased

(B) decrease taxes when the money supply is decreased

(C) increase government spending when the money supply is decreased

(D) increase taxes when interest rates are increased

(E) decrease taxes when interest rates are increased

52. Which of the following policy changes are most appropriate to address a severe recession?

    (A) Decreasing the money supply and increasing taxes
    (B) Increasing the discount rate and taxes
    (C) Decreasing government spending and taxes by the same amount
    (D) Increasing government transfers and buying U.S. Treasury bonds
    (E) Keeping the money supply constant while reducing the budget deficit

53. Which of the following fiscal and monetary policy combinations would most likely result in an increase in aggregate demand?

	Government Spending	Reserve Requirement	Open-Market Operations
(A)	Increase	Decrease	Sell bonds
(B)	Increase	Decrease	Buy bonds
(C)	Decrease	Increase	Sell bonds
(D)	Increase	Increase	Buy bonds
(E)	Decrease	Decrease	Buy bonds

54. Which of the following changes will likely cause an increase in both aggregate demand and aggregate supply?

    (A) An increase in labor productivity
    (B) A decrease in input prices
    (C) A decrease in personal income tax rates
    (D) A decrease in business tax rates
    (E) An increase in investment spending

55. A contractionary fiscal policy combined with an expansionary fiscal policy will necessarily result in

    (A) an increase in gross domestic product
    (B) a decrease in gross domestic product
    (C) an increase in interest rates
    (D) a decrease in interest rates
    (E) a federal budget deficit

56. If a contractionary monetary policy is followed by an expansionary fiscal policy, how will the nominal interest rate and the unemployment rate likely be affected in the short-run?

	Nominal Interest Rate	Unemployment
(A)	Increase	Decrease
(B)	Decrease	Increase
(C)	Indeterminate	Indeterminate
(D)	Increase	Indeterminate
(E)	Decrease	Decrease

57. A reduction of unemployment can best be achieved by which of the following combinations of fiscal and monetary policy?

	Fiscal Policy	Monetary Policy
(A)	Increase taxes	Increase reserve requirements
(B)	Decrease taxes	Raise discount rate
(C)	Increase government spending	Buy government bonds
(D)	Increase government spending	Sell government bonds
(E)	Decrease government spending	Buy government bonds

TOPIC 4: GOVERNMENT DEFICITS AND DEBT

DIFFICULTY LEVEL 2

58. The government budget balance equals

(A) Government spending – taxes + government transfers

(B) Taxes – government spending + government transfers

(C) Taxes – government spending – government transfers

(D) Taxes + government spending + government transfers

(E) Government transfers – government spending – taxes

59. Federal budget deficits occur when

    (A) Congress increases the tax rate for households earning the highest incomes
    (B) an increase in unemployment causes government transfers to increase
    (C) the Internal Revenue Service spends more than it collects in a given year
    (D) the federal government spends more than it collects in taxes in a given year
    (E) the Federal Reserve increases the money supply

60. An expansionary fiscal policy enacted by the United States government

    (A) always includes a change in taxes.
    (B) moves the federal budget toward deficit.
    (C) moves the federal budget toward surplus.
    (D) moves the federal budget toward balance.
    (E) only affects government spending.

61. Deficit spending by the United States government is primarily financed by

    (A) decreasing the discount rate
    (B) increasing the money supply
    (C) depreciating the value of the dollar
    (D) increasing taxes
    (E) issuing new bonds

62. An increase in government spending with no change in taxes leads to a(n)

    (A) decrease in income
    (B) increase in interest rates
    (C) increase in the money supply
    (D) decrease in bond prices
    (E) increase in unemployment

63. Which of the following statements is true about the national debt of the United States?

   (A) It can never be fully paid.
   (B) It increases when full employment output increases.
   (C) It is the net result of past and current budget deficits and surpluses.
   (D) It is owed entirely to foreign investors.
   (E) It is owed entirely to domestic commercial banks.

64. In an economy at full employment, policymakers are concerned about the government debt and attempt to decrease it by reducing government spending and transfers and increasing income taxes. Which of the following will most likely increase as a result of these policies?

   (A) Price level
   (B) Labor productivity
   (C) Aggregate supply
   (D) Nominal wages
   (E) Unemployment

65. Which of the following will cause a government budget deficit in a given year?

   (A) Tax revenues are less than government spending and transfers.
   (B) Capital outflows to foreign economies exceed capital inflows from foreign economies.
   (C) The central bank increases bond purchases.
   (D) Interest payments on the national debt exceed spending on goods and services.
   (E) The value of imports exceeds the value of exports.

66. To finance a budget deficit, the U.S. government will most likely

   (A) issue bonds to borrow money
   (B) increase taxes
   (C) sell physical assets
   (D) seize assets from foreign nations
   (E) increase interest rates on financial aid to developing nations

67. How do automatic stabilizers affect the government budget balance as the United States' economy moves toward recession?

(A) Lawmakers increase government spending and the budget moves toward deficit

(B) Tax rates increase and the budget moves toward surplus

(C) Tax rates decrease and the budget moves toward deficit

(D) Increasing transfer payments move the budget toward deficit

(E) Decreasing transfer payments move the budget toward surplus

68. How will an increase in the government budget deficit likely affect the real interest rates and investment spending?

	Real Interest Rate	Investment Spending
(A)	Increase	Increase
(B)	Increase	Decrease
(C)	No change	No change
(D)	Decrease	Increase
(E)	Decrease	Decrease

THE PHILLIPS CURVE

TOPIC 1: SHORT-RUN AND LONG-RUN PHILLIPS CURVES

DIFFICULTY LEVEL 2

Use the graph below to answer the following question.

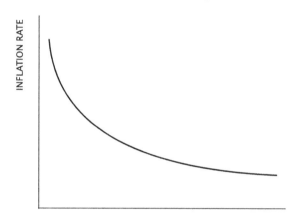

UNEMPLOYMENT RATE

1. Which curve is depicted in the graph above?

   (A) Production possibilities curve

   (B) Aggregate demand curve

   (C) Short-run Phillips curve

   (D) Long-run Phillips curve

   (E) Short-run aggregate supply curve

2. According to the short-run Phillips curve, as the inflation rate decreases

   (A) the unemployment rate increases
   (B) the labor force participation rate increases
   (C) the government budget deficit increases
   (D) real gross domestic product increases
   (E) nominal wages decrease

3. According to the short-run Phillips curve, a high rate of inflation is associated with

   (A) a low real interest rate
   (B) a high unemployment rate
   (C) a low unemployment rate
   (D) a decreasing money supply
   (E) a low reserve ratio

Use the graph below to answer the following questions.

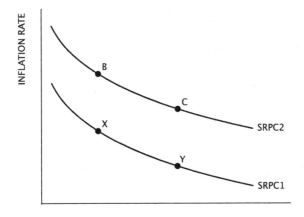

4. An increase in aggregate demand will cause a movement from point

   (A) X to B
   (B) B to X
   (C) X to Y
   (D) Y to X
   (E) Y to B

5. If the Federal Reserve implements a contractionary monetary policy, how will this policy be reflected in the graph above?

   (A) A movement from Point B to Point C
   (B) A movement from Point C to Point B
   (C) A shift of SRPC1 to SRPC2
   (D) A shift of SRPC2 to SRPC1
   (E) The short-run Phillips curve will be unaffected

6. A leftward shift of the short-run Phillips curve is most likely due to

   (A) an increase in nominal wages
   (B) a decrease in worker productivity
   (C) a decrease in the price of oil
   (D) a increase in the money supply
   (E) an increase in consumption spending

7. Which of the following is true of the Phillips curve?

   (A) It is upward sloping in the short-run and downward sloping in the long-run.
   (B) It is downward sloping in the short-run and vertical in the long-run.
   (C) It represents the trade-off between unemployment and output in the short-run.
   (D) It is vertical in the short-run and downward sloping in the short-run.
   (E) It is vertical in the long-run at a fixed rate of inflation.

8. Which of the following changes could cause a movement along the short-run Phillips curve toward higher inflation and lower unemployment?

    (A) An improvement in the quality of capital goods

    (B) An increase in human capital

    (C) An increase in savings by the country's consumers

    (D) An increase in exports

    (E) An increase in marginal corporate taxes

9. Which of the following is true of the long-run Phillips curve?

    (A) It will shift if there is a change in aggregate demand.

    (B) It represents an indirect relationship between inflation and unemployment.

    (C) It represents a direct relationship between inflation and unemployment.

    (D) It is vertical at the natural rate of unemployment.

    (E) It represents the cyclical rate of unemployment.

10. How will an increase in nominal wages affect the short-run Phillips curve and the long-run Phillips curve?

	Short-run aggregate supply	Long-run Phillips curve
(A)	Shift to the right	Shift to the right
(B)	Shift to the right	Shift to the left
(C)	Shift to the right	No change
(D)	Shift to the left	Shift to the right
(E)	Shift to the left	No change

Use the graph below to answer the following questions.

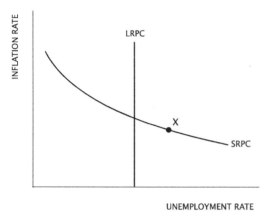

11. Assuming that the economy depicted in the graph above is currently operating at Point X on the short-run Phillips curve, which of the following is true?

(A) The current unemployment rate is equal to the natural rate of unemployment.
(B) The current unemployment rate is equal to the non-accelerating inflation rate of unemployment (NAIRU).
(C) Current output is greater than full-employment output.
(D) The economy is in recession.
(E) The inflation rate is increasing.

12. Assuming that the economy depicted in the graph above is currently operating at Point X, how will the economy change in the long-run?

(A) The unemployment rate will increase
(B) The unemployment rate will be equal to the natural rate of unemployment
(C) The inflation rate will increase
(D) The long-run Phillips curve will shift to the right
(E) Short-run aggregate supply will decrease

Use the graph below to answer the following question.

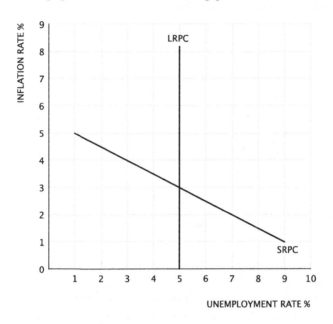

13. According to the graph above, the natural rate of unemployment is

(A) 1 percent

(B) 3 percent

(C) 5 percent

(D) 9 percent

(E) indeterminate

14. According to the graph above, if the unemployment rate is currently 4 percent, then

(A) the economy is in recession

(B) the current unemployment rate is greater than the natural rate

(C) the short-run Phillips curve will shift to the left

(D) the inflation rate will increase in the long-run

(E) the inflation rate will remain constant

Use the graph below to answer the following question.

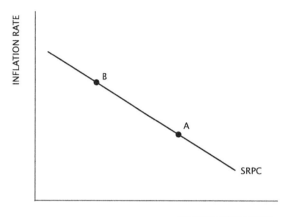

15. Which of the following changes will most likely cause a movement from Point A to Point B on the short-run Phillips curve in the graph above?

(A) Increase in personal income taxes

(B) Increase in domestic military expenditures

(C) Increase in the global supply of oil

(D) Increase in inflationary expectations

(E) Increase in the required reserve ratio

DIFFICULTY LEVEL 2

16. Which of the following will cause demand-pull inflation?

   (A) An increase in short-run aggregate supply
   (B) An increase in long-run aggregate supply
   (C) An increase in aggregate demand
   (D) A decrease in aggregate demand
   (E) A decrease in short-run aggregate supply

Use the graph below to answer the following question.

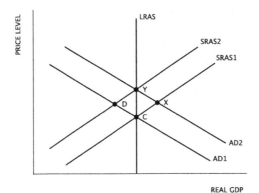

17. Starting with equilibrium point C, which of the following shifts of equilibrium identifies the short-run and the long-run results of a demand-pull inflation?

	Short-run	Long-run
(A)	C to X	X to C
(B)	C to Y	Y to X
(C)	C to D	D to Y
(D)	C to X	X to Y
(E)	C to Y	Y to C

18. Assuming the economy is at full employment, which of the following will most likely result in demand-pull inflation in the short run?

   (A) A decrease in consumption spending
   (B) An increase in household savings
   (C) A decrease in the real interest rate
   (D) A drought that affects the entire nation
   (E) An increase in the demand for cell phones

19. Which of the following changes will most likely cause cost-push inflation?

   (A) An increase in government spending
   (B) Crowding out
   (C) An increase in frictional unemployment
   (D) Deflation
   (E) An increase in the prices of steel and coal

20. Assuming the government uses fiscal policy to reduce demand-pull inflation, which of the following changes will most likely result?

   (A) An increasing government budget deficit
   (B) An increase in the unemployment rate
   (C) An increase in nominal wages
   (D) A decrease in private investment spending
   (E) An increase in real gross domestic product

21. When an economy is at full employment, which of the following will most likely create cost-push inflation in the short-run?

   (A) The Federal Reserve increases bond purchases
   (B) Lawmakers increase personal income taxes
   (C) Lawmakers decrease the corporate tax rate
   (D) Labor unions win widespread increases in nominal wages
   (E) Industries implement more efficient automated production methods

DIFFICULTY LEVEL 2

22. Which of the following changes will likely occur if there is an increase in the expected rate of inflation?

    (A) An increase in short-run aggregate supply
    (B) A decrease in long-run aggregate supply
    (C) A rightward shift of the long-run Phillips curve
    (D) A leftward shift of the short-run Phillips curve
    (E) A rightward shift of the short-run Phillips curve

23. Which of the following changes will cause a rightward shift in the short-run Phillips curve?

    (A) an increase in aggregate supply
    (B) an increase in the expected rate of inflation
    (C) a decrease in the expected rate of inflation
    (D) an increase in aggreagate demand
    (E) a decrease in aggregate demand

24. Which of the following changes will lead to a decrease in the expected rate of inflation?

    (A) A decrease in income tax rates
    (B) An increase in the marginal propensity to consume
    (C) An increase in the prices of productive inputs
    (D) An increase in exports
    (E) A decrease in the money supply

25. According to rational expectations theory, people

    (A) use all available information in forming their expectations about future inflation

    (B) assume that future inflation will be the same as past inflation

    (C) base expectations about future inflation exclusively on historical data

    (D) do not estimate future inflation rates

    (E) predict that future inflation will not change from current levels

26. Which of the following changes may result in an increase in inflation and unemployment?

    (A) Increased purchases of capital goods

    (B) An increase in consumer spending

    (C) A decrease in the marginal propensity to save

    (D) An increase in inflationary expectations

    (E) A decrease in the price of productive resources

27. Assume that the Federal Reserve implements an expansionary monetary policy. If workers believe that this policy will cause inflation and demand higher wages, they are following the principles of

    (A) the Phillips effect

    (B) adaptive expectations

    (C) rational expectations

    (D) the quantity theory of money

    (E) the money multiplier effect

28. According to the rational expectations theory, an announced increase in the money supply will have which of the following effects on nominal and real gross domestic product (GDP)?

	Nominal GDP	Real GDP
(A)	Increase	Increase
(B)	Increase	Decrease
(C)	Increase	No change
(D)	Decrease	Increase
(E)	No change	Increase

29. According to rational expectations theory, which of the following will result if households and firms anticipate an expansionary monetary policy?

(A) An increase in cyclical unemployment

(B) An increase in nominal gross domestic output

(C) A decrease in real gross domestic output

(D) A decrease in the price level

(E) A decrease in the natural rate of unemployment

Economic Growth

DEFINITION OF ECONOMIC GROWTH

DIFFICULTY LEVEL 2

1. An increase in a country's standard of living is best indicated by an increase in

   (A) employment
   (B) real gross domestic product per capita
   (C) real gross domestic product
   (D) nominal gross domestic product
   (E) price level

2. In a given year, if real gross domestic product grows by 10% while the population grows by 9% then

   (A) the economy is in recession
   (B) the inflation rate is increasing
   (C) real gross domestic product per capita is increasing
   (D) the unemployment rate is decreasing
   (E) the standard of living is decreasing

3. Which of the following best defines economic growth?

   (A) An increase in short-run aggregate supply
   (B) A decrease in structural unemployment
   (C) A sustained increase in real gross domestic product
   (D) An increase in aggregate output
   (E) An increase in the labor force participation rate

4. Which of the following statements concerning economic growth is true?

   (A) The economic growth rate will decrease if firms increase purchases of capital goods

   (B) Long-run economic growth results in an increase in aggregate supply

   (C) Real gross domestic product per capita increases as the population increases

   (D) Economic growth necessarily increases the standard of living of the average citizen

   (E) Economic growth causes an increase in the personal wealth of every citizen

Use the graph below to answer the following question.

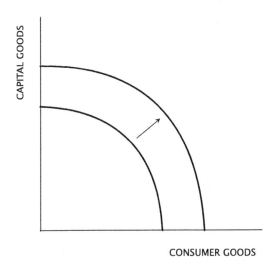

CONSUMER GOODS

5. The change indicated by the arrow in the production possibilities graph above indicates which of the following?

   (A) An increase in net exports

   (B) Economic growth

   (C) An increase in the inflation rate

   (D) An expansionary fiscal policy

   (E) An increase in aggregate demand

Use the graph below to answer the following question.

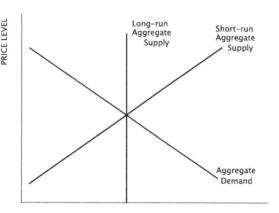

REAL GROSS DOMESTIC PRODUCT

6. How can economic growth be indicated on the graph above?

   (A) A rightward shift of aggregate demand
   (B) A rightward shift of short-run aggregate supply
   (C) A rightward shift of long-run aggregate supply
   (D) A leftward shift of long-run aggregate supply
   (E) An upward shift of short-run aggregate supply

7. Which of the following statements describes an improvement in a country's standard of living?

   (A) Prices fall in the short-run
   (B) Foreign currencies can purchase more domestic currency
   (C) Population decreases at a faster rate than a decrease in long-run aggregate supply
   (D) Taxes increase at a faster rate than short-run aggregate supply
   (E) Imports decrease at a faster rate than a decrease in exports

Use the graph below to answer the following question.

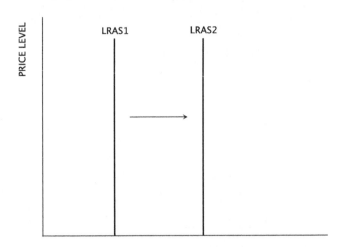

8. Which of the following is represented by the change in the graph above?

    (A) An increase in aggregate price level
    (B) An increase in potential output
    (C) An increase in government spending
    (D) A decrease in short-run aggregate supply
    (E) A decrease in full employment output

9. Which of the following indicates economic growth?

    I.   A rightward shift of short-run aggregate supply
    II. A rightward shift of long-run aggregate supply
    III. An outward shift of the production possibilities curve

    (A) I only
    (B) II only
    (C) III only
    (D) I and III only
    (E) II and III only

DETERMINANTS OF ECONOMIC GROWTH

TOPIC 3: RESEARCH AND DEVELOPMENT AND TECHNOLOGICAL PROGRESS

DIFFICULTY LEVEL 2

1. An increase in which of the following is most likely to cause economic growth?

    (A) Consumption spending
    (B) Educational attainment of the population
    (C) Money supply
    (D) Corporate taxes
    (E) Structural unemployment

2. An increase in which of the following will most likely cause economic growth in the long run?

    (A) Consumption of consumer goods
    (B) Money supply
    (C) Inflation rate
    (D) Population
    (E) Imports

3. Which of the following factors can affect economic growth?

    I. The quantity and quality of a country's labor force
    II. The level of technology
    III. The quantity and quality of capital goods

    (A) I only.
    (B) III only.
    (C) I and III only.
    (D) II and III only.
    (E) I, II, and III.

4. Which of the following would increase attainment of human capital?

    (A) Implementation of new technology
    (B) An increase in financial aid for college students
    (C) Purchases of new productive machinery
    (D) An increase in the labor force participation rate
    (E) A decrease in the unemployment rate

5. The replacement of hand-operated machinery with automated production machinery is an example of

    (A) an improvement in human capital
    (B) an increase in the supply of consumption goods
    (C) an investment in capital goods and technology
    (D) decreasing productivity
    (E) a decrease in physical capital

6. Productivity is affected by each of the following EXCEPT

    (A) Investment in physical capital
    (B) Vocational training
    (C) The size of the labor force
    (D) The price of natural resources
    (E) Technological progress

7. Which changes to capital per worker and output per worker result in the greatest increase in economic growth?

	Capital per worker	Output per worker
(A)	Increase	Increase
(B)	Decrease	Increase
(C)	No change	No change
(D)	Increase	Decrease
(E)	Decrease	Increase

8. Which of the following would most likely cause economic growth?

   (A) Increased consumption spending
   (B) Increased government spending
   (C) Decreased wages
   (D) Technological progress
   (E) Increased real interest rates

GROWTH POLICY

DIFFICULTY LEVEL 2

1. An increase in which of the following is most likely to result in economic growth?

   (A) Real interest rates

   (B) The required reserve ratio

   (C) Investment tax credits

   (D) That natural rate of unemployment

   (E) The government budget deficit

Use the graph below to answer the following question.

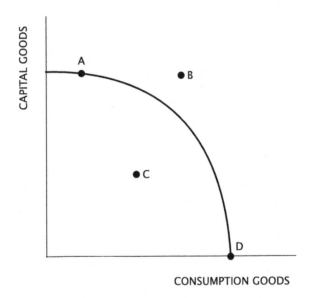

CONSUMPTION GOODS

2. All of the following statements about this economy are true EXCEPT

    (A) Point C represents an inefficient level of production

    (B) Point D represents the most efficient level of consumption goods production

    (C) Production at Point A will lead to more economic growth than production at Point D

    (D) Point A represents the best use of resources for this economy

    (E) Point B repesents a level of production that is unattainable with current resources

3. Which government action will most likely increase long-run economic growth?

    (A) An increase in unemployment benefits

    (B) A decrease in government expenditures

    (C) An increase in import tariffs

    (D) A decrease in personal income taxes

    (E) An increase in subsidies to businesses for purchases of capital goods

4. Assuming that national savings increases in an economy, what will be the likely result on investment spending and economic growth?

	Investment Spending	Economic Growth
(A)	Increase	Increase
(B)	Increase	Decrease
(C)	Decrease	Increase
(D)	Decrease	Decrease
(E)	No change	No change

5. Suppose that a national government increased deficit spending on goods and services. In the long run, how will this policy affect the real interest rate and investment spending?

	Real Interest Rate	Investment Spending
(A)	Increase	No change
(B)	Increase	Decrease
(C)	No change	No change
(D)	Decrease	Increase
(E)	Decrease	Decrease

6. If an economy is experiencing a recession but policymakers desire to support long-run economic growth, which combination of fiscal and monetary policy is most appropriate?

	Fiscal Policy	Monetary Policy
(A)	Increase taxes	Buy bonds
(B)	Decrease government spending	Sell bonds
(C)	Decrease taxes	Buy bonds
(D)	Decrease government spending	Sell bonds
(E)	No change	Buy bonds

7. An increase in which of the following would likely hinder economic growth?

(A) Spending on technological research and development

(B) The government budget deficit

(C) Private investment

(D) The marginal propensity to save

(E) Bond purchases by the central bank

Open Economy: International Trade and Finance

BALANCE OF PAYMENTS ACCOUNTS

TOPIC 1: BALANCE OF TRADE

DIFFICULTY LEVEL 2

1. If an economy sells more goods and services to the rest of the world than it purchases from the rest of the world then that economy has a

   (A) trade deficit
   (B) trade surplus
   (C) trade balance
   (D) budget deficit
   (E) budget surplus

2. Which of the following will increase the trade deficit of the United States?

   (A) South American citizens increasing tourist visits to the United States
   (B) United States firms buying capital goods from Japan
   (C) The United States selling 1 million tons of soy to India
   (D) The United States dollar depreciating in the foreign exchange market
   (E) A United States company being hired to perform environmental services in China

3. If consumers buy more domestic goods and fewer imported goods, how will the trade balance move and how will equilibrium income be affected?

	Trade Balance	Equilibrium Income
(A)	Toward deficit	Increases
(B)	Toward deficit	Decreases
(C)	Toward surplus	Increases
(D)	Toward surplus	Decreases
(E)	Toward surplus	Is unaffected

4. Which of the following will most likely cause an increased deficit in an economy's balance of trade?

(A) A decrease in tariffs imposed by its trading partners

(B) Rising imports and declining exports

(C) An increase in the domestic price level relative to its trading partners

(D) A depreciating currency

(E) A decrease in capital inflow

5. There will be a decrease in the United States trade deficit if there is an increase in

(A) United States demand for Chinese goods

(B) The value of foreign currency relative to the U.S. dollar

(C) The federal budget deficit

(D) U.S. interest rates relative to other countries

(E) The price level in the U.S. relative to other countries

DIFFICULTY LEVEL 2

6. Which of the following would be a current account transaction?

    (A) A United States firm builds a retail store in the United Arab Emirates.
    (B) China buys United States Treasury bonds.
    (C) A South Korean manufacturer pays a U.S. company to ship goods overseas
    (D) The United States Federal Reserve purchases Chinese currency
    (E) A Canadian firm purchases stock in a United States corporation

7. Which of the following transactions is NOT counted in the current account in the United States balance of payments?

    (A) A United States firm purchases mining equipment from a Japanese manufacturer.
    (B) An Argentinian investor receives a dividend payment from a United States corporation.
    (C) United States consumers purchase computer equipment made in China.
    (D) An immigrant in the United States sends money to her family in Ecuador.
    (E) A Swedish corporation purchases a lumber corporation in the United States.

8. The current account includes which of the following transactions?

    I.   An American restaurant owner buys cheese from an Italian cheesemaker.
    II. An Italian auto corporation purchases stock in an American auto corporation.
    III. An American auto corporation pays a dividend to Italian stockholders.

    (A) I only.
    (B) II only.
    (C) I and II only.
    (D) I and III only.
    (E) I, II, and III.

9. If an economy has a current account deficit, there will be a

   (A) government budget surplus

   (B) deficit in the balance of payments

   (C) deficit in the financial account

   (D) surplus in the financial account

   (E) balance of trade surplus

TOPIC 3: FINANCIAL ACCOUNT

DIFFICULTY LEVEL 2

10. Which of the following is an example of foreign direct investment?

    (A) A United States citizen purchasing corporate bonds issued by a Dutch firm

    (B) A Japanese financial institution purchasing U.S. dollars

    (C) A German appliance manufacturer building an assembly plant in the United States

    (D) The Chinese central bank purchasing United States Treasury bills

    (E) An immigrant worker in the United States sending money to his native country

11. The purchase of corporate bonds issued by a French corporation by Chinese investors will be included in China's

    (A) financial account

    (B) current account

    (C) imports

    (D) foreign direct investment

    (E) trade deficit

12. Suppose an American furniture company purchases a manufacturing plant in Indonesia. This purchase is included in Indonesia's

   (A) financial account
   (B) current account
   (C) surplus account
   (D) imports
   (E) balance of trade

FOREIGN EXCHANGE MARKET

TOPIC 1: DEMAND FOR AND SUPPLY OF FOREIGN EXCHANGE

DIFFICULTY LEVEL 2

1. Suppose that the United States and China are the only trading partners in the world. If the U.S. lowers import restrictions from China, then
    (A) the demand for U.S. dollars will increase, appreciating the dollar
    (B) the demand for Chinese yuan will increase, appreciating the yuan
    (C) the demand for Chinese yuan will increase, appreciating the dollar
    (D) the supply of U.S. dollars will increase, appreciating the dollar
    (E) the demand for Chinese yuan will decrease, appreciating the dollar

Use the graph below to answer the following questions.

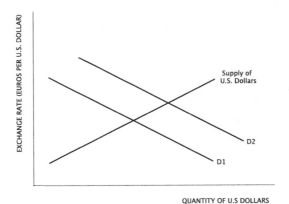

2. According to the graph, a shift from D1 to D2 represents

   (A) an increase in demand for euros

   (B) an increase in demand for U.S. dollars

   (C) an increase in supply of U.S. dollars

   (D) a decrease in demand for euros

   (E) a decrease in demand for U.S. dollars

3. Which of the following causes the shift from D1 to D2 depicted in the graph?

   (A) An increase in the United States' demand for European goods

   (B) An increase in the price level in the United States

   (C) A decrease in the price level in Europe

   (D) A decrease in United States tariffs on European goods

   (E) United States interest rates are higher than European interest rates

4. How is the supply of and demand for United States dollars affected by an increase in purchases of capital goods by American companies in India?

	Supply of U.S. dollars	Demand for U.S. dollars
(A)	Increase	Increase
(B)	Increase	Decrease
(C)	Increase	No change
(D)	Decrease	Increase
(E)	No change	Decrease

5. Which of the following changes will occur in the foreign exchange market for United States dollars if investors in the United States and in other nations increase their purchases of United States financial assets such as stocks and bonds?

	Demand for U.S. dollars	Supply of U.S. dollars
(A)	Increase	Increase
(B)	Decrease	Increase
(C)	No change	Increase
(D)	Increase	Decrease
(E)	Increase	No change

6. Assuming American tourists increase their visits to Brazil, how will the foreign exchange markets for the U.S. dollar and the Brazilian real be affected?

   (A) The supply of the U.S dollar will increase and the supply of the Brazilian real will decrease

   (B) The demand for both currencies will increase

   (C) The supply of the U.S. dollar will increase and the demand for the Brazilian real will increase

   (D) The supply of both currencies will increase

   (E) The demand for the U.S. dollar will increase and the supply of the Brazilian real will increase

7. Suppose that Russia, whose currency is the ruble, is experiencing high inflation relative to the United States, whose currency is the dollar. Which of the following would occur in the foreign exchange market?

   (A) An increase in the demand for the Russian ruble

   (B) An increase in the demand for the U.S. dollar

   (C) A decrease in the demand for the U.S. dollar

   (D) An decrease in the supply of the Russian ruble

   (E) No change in the supply of the Russian ruble

8. Suppose that Britain and the United States were the only trading partners in the world. If the income of British citizens increases relative to income of American citizens, there will likely be an increase in which of the following?

   (A) Demand for the British pound and the supply of U.S. dollars

   (B) Demand for both British pounds and U.S. dollars

   (C) Supply of both British pounds and U.S. dollars

   (D) Supply of the British pound and demand for the U.S. dollar

   (E) Exports from Britain and imports to the U.S.

DIFFICULTY LEVEL 1

9. Which of the following refers to the price of one economy's currency expressed in terms of another economy's currency?

(A) Real interest rate

(B) Nominal interest rate

(C) Comparative advantage

(D) Exchange rate

(E) Terms of trade

DIFFICULTY LEVEL 2

Use the graph below to answer the following question.

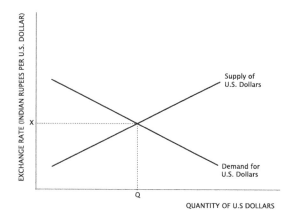

10. According to the graph, how will the supply of U.S. dollars and the exchange rate be affected by an increase in investment spending in India by United States firms?

	Supply of U.S. Dollars	Exchange Rate
(A)	Leftward shift	Increase
(B)	Leftward shift	Decrease
(C)	Rightward shift	Increase
(D)	Rightward shift	Decrease
(E)	No change	No change

11. Which of the following changes will occur in the foreign exchange market for United States dollars if investors from abroad increase their purchases of U.S. government bonds?

	Demand for U.S. dollars	Value of U.S. dollar
(A)	Increase	No change
(B)	Decrease	Depreciates
(C)	No change	No change
(D)	Increase	Appreciates
(E)	Increase	Depreciates

12. An increase in exports from the United States to nations overseas will result in which of the following in foreign exchange markets?

(A) A increase in the value of the United States dollar

(B) An increased supply of the United States dollar

(C) Decreased United States demand for foreign currencies

(D) An increase in the value of foreign currencies

(E) A decrease in foreign demand for United States dollars

13. Assume that the inflation rate in Venezuela is very high relative to the inflation rates in all of its trading partners. Which of the following is likely to happen to Venezuela's currency, the bolivar, on the foreign exchange market?

(A) Demand for the Venezuelan bolivar will increase, and the currency will appreciate
(B) Demand for the Venezuelan bolivar will decrease, and the currency will depreciate
(C) Demand for the Venezuelan bolivar will not change, but the currency will depreciate
(D) The supply of the Venezuelan bolivar will decrease, and the currency will appreciate
(E) The supply of the Venezuelan bolivar will decrease, and the currency will depreciate

14. A depreciation of the Mexican peso on the foreign exchange market could be caused by an increase in which of the following?

(A) Purchases of Mexican goods and services by its trading partners
(B) Foreign tariffs on Mexican goods exported to its trading partners
(C) Mexican interest rates
(D) Inflation rates among Mexico's trading partners
(E) Demand for the Mexican peso

15. Which of the following changes will likely cause an appreciation in the value of the U.S. dollar on the foreign exchange market?

(A) Interest rates in Canada increase relative to interest rates in the United States
(B) Americans begin to prefer domestically produced goods to foreign-produced goods
(C) Inflation rates in the United States rise relative to its trading partners
(D) American currency speculators increase their purchases of Asian currencies
(E) American oil refineries increase their demand for crude oil from Saudi Arabia

Use the graph below to answer the following question.

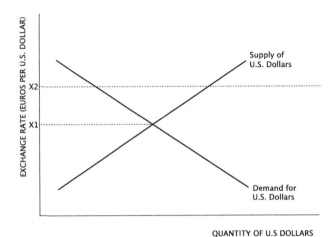

16. According to the graph, which of the following changes will result in a change in the exchange rate from X1 to X2?

    (A) American investors speculate that the euro will increase in value

    (B) European-made fashions grow in popularity among Americans

    (C) American manufacturers shift production to European factories

    (D) The inflation rate in the United States increases relative to Europe

    (E) U.S. Treasury bonds increase in value relative to European financial assets

DIFFICULTY LEVEL 2

17. An increase in the value of the United States dollar on foreign exchange markets will most likely benefit

(A) German citizens who desire to purchase real estate in the United States

(B) U.S. restaurant owners who regularly import French and Chilean wine

(C) South Korean tourists on vacation in the United States

(D) A retired Italian living in the United States who receives Italian pension checks

(E) A U.S. auto producer who sells cars and trucks overseas

18. Which of the following will lead to a depreciation of a nation's currency?

(A) An increased demand for the nation's currency

(B) Decreased real interest rates in the nation compared with the rest of the world

(C) An increase in exports

(D) A lower price level in the nation relative to the rest of the world

(E) A decreased demand for imports among the nation's citizens

19. The value of a country's currency will tend to appreciate if

(A) demand for the country's exports decreases

(B) foreigners investors speculate that the country's currency will increase in value

(C) the country's firms increase their investment spending abroad

(D) domestic inflation rates increase

(E) the country's citizens increase their purchases of foreign goods

20. Which of the following is true if price level has been rising in Canada relative to the price level in the United States?

(A) The Canadian dollar will have appreciated relative to the United States dollar.

(B) The Canadian dollar will have depreciated relative to the United States dollar.

(C) Canada is experiencing a recession while the United States economy is experiencing growth

(D) The United States' money supply is growing at a faster rate than Canada's

(E) Real interest rates are increasing in the United States relative to Canada'

21. Which of the following would cause the Mexican peso to appreciate relative to the
     United States dollar?

(A) An increase in Mexico's inflation rate

(B) An increase in Mexico's interest rates relative to the United States' interest rates

(C) An increase in Mexican household income

(D) An increase in United States household income

(E) An increase in Mexico's imports

22. Which of the following will benefit from a depreciation of the United States dollar on the
     foreign exchange market?

(A) An American firm that sells services to customers abroad

(B) A Swedish firm that sells services to customers in the United States

(C) An American investor intending to purchase a factory in China

(D) An Indian computer programmer hired by a firm in the United States

(E) A German firm that sells goods exclusively in Europe

23. If Chinese firms and citizens increase their investment in the United States, the supply
     of Chinese yuan to the foreign exchange market and the dollar price of the yuan will
     likely change in which of the following ways?

	Supply of Chinese Yuan	Dollar Price of Yuan
(A)	Increase	Increase
(B)	Increase	Decrease
(C)	Decrease	Increase
(D)	Decrease	Decrease
(E)	Decrease	No change

24. If the international value of the United States dollar depreciates in comparison to the
     European Union's euro currency, which of the following is likely to occur?

(A) The United States government will enact trade quotas on European imports.

(B) Trade between the United States and Europe will not be affected.

(C) United States exports to Europe will increase.

(D) The United States will increase its balance of trade deficit with Europe.

(E)   United States investors will increase purchases of European financial assets

IMPORTS, EXPORTS, AND FINANCIAL CAPITAL FLOWS

DIFFICULTY LEVEL 2

1. Assume that the real interest rate in the United States increases relative to that of the rest of the world. Which of the following is most likely to result?

   (A) United States consumers will increase their demand for imported goods
   (B) Firms in the United States will increase purchases of foreign capital goods
   (C) The United States government will increase tariffs on imported goods
   (D) Capital will flow into the United States from the rest of the world
   (E) United States citizens will increase purchases of foreign financial assets

2. Assume the United States and China are the only trading partners in the world. If the real interest rate in the United States decreases relative to that of China, capital flow and the value of the U.S. currency should change in which of the following ways?

	Capital flow	Value of U.S. currency
(A)	Out of U.S.	Appreciate
(B)	Out of U.S.	Depreciate
(C)	Out of U.S.	No change
(D)	Into U.S.	Appreciate
(E)	Into U.S.	Depreciate

3. Which of the following is a likely result of an appreciation of the United States dollar?

   (A) United States imports will increase
   (B) United States exports will increase
   (C) United States goods will become less expensive in foreign markets
   (D) Demand for the United States dollar will increase
   (E) The United States government will pursue a fixed exchange rate

4. Assume that there is a decrease in the real interest rate, followed by an increase in financial capital outflows from the United States. How will the increase in capital ouflows likely affect net exports and aggregate demand in the United States?

Net Exports	Aggregate Demand

(A)	Decrease	Decrease
(B)	Decrease	No change
(C)	Increase	Increase
(D)	Increase	Decrease
(E)	Increase	No change

5. Supposing that the Federal Reserve pursues a contractionary monetary policy, what will happen to the international value of the dollar, United States imports, and United States exports?

	International Value of U.S. Dollar	U.S. Imports	U.S. Exports
(A)	Appreciation	Decrease	Increase
(B)	Depreciation	Decrease	Increase
(C)	Depreciation	Increase	Decrease
(D)	Appreciation	Increase	Decrease
(E)	No change	No change	No change

6. Assume that Japanese consumers increase their demand for United States financial assets. How would the international supply of Japanese yen, the value of the U.S. dollar relative to the Japanese yen, and Japanese net exports to the United States change?

	Supply of Japanese Yen	Value of U.S. Dollar	Japanese Net Exports
(A)	Increase	Increase	Increase
(B)	Increase	Increase	Decrease
(C)	Increase	Decrease	Decrease
(D)	Decrease	Decrease	Decrease
(E)	No change	Decrease	Increase

7. If the Federal Reserve pursues an expansionary monetary policy to reduce interest rates, how will international capital flows be affected?

(A) Short-run capital inflows to the United States will not change.

(B) Short-run capital inflows to the United States will decrease.

(C) Short-run capital inflows to the United States will increase.

(D) Short-run capital outflows from the United States will decrease.

(E) Long-run capital inflows to the United States will increase.

8. Suppose that the supply of loanable funds increases in Mexico, whose currency is the peso. The international value of the peso and Mexico's exports will most likely change in which of the following ways?

	International value of the peso	Mexico's exports
(A)	Increases	Increase
(B)	Increases	Decrease
(C)	Decreases	Increase
(D)	Decreases	Decrease
(E)	No change	No change

RELATIONSHIPS BETWEEN INTERNATIONAL AND DOMESTIC FINANCIAL AND GOODS MARKETS

DIFFICULTY LEVEL 2

1. Which of the following is a likely result of an appreciation of the United States dollar?

   (A) United States imports will increase
   (B) United States exports will increase
   (C) United States goods will become less expensive in foreign markets
   (D) Demand for the United States dollar will increase
   (E) The United States government will pursue a fixed exchange rate

2. What is the main benefit of the removal of trade restrictions between two countries?

   (A) Output in each country will increase
   (B) Each country will become more self-sufficient
   (C) Each country can consume beyond its constraints of resources and productivity
   (D) Investment spending will increase in each country
   (E) Unemployment will decrease in each country

3. Which of the following benefits from a United States tariff on imported goods?

   (A) An American retailer of appliances made in Japan
   (B) A German automobile manufacturer facing competition from American auto companies
   (C) An American producer of microchips facing competition from Chinese manufacturers
   (D) American consumers of goods imported from abroad
   (E) Americans who purchase stocks in Japanese stock markets

4. Which of the following will most likely benefit from a depreciation of the United States dollar in the short run?

   (A) American consumers buying European goods
   (B) Chinese investors holding United States bonds

(C) Japanese exporters of goods to the United States

(D) American tourists traveling to France

(E) Canadian firms that purchase capital goods from the United States

5. Which of the following would most likely result if the United States increased tariffs on imported goods?

(A) Exports from the United States would increase

(B) The standard of living in the United States would increase

(C) Foreign producers of goods would benefit

(D) The United States economy would become less efficient

(E) Full employment output in the United States would increase in the long-run

6. How will an increase in the government's budget deficit affect the exchange rate and net exports?

	Exchange Rate	Net Exports
(A)	Appreciate	Increase
(B)	Appreciate	Decrease
(C)	Appreciate	No change
(D)	Depreciate	Increase
(E)	Depreciate	Decrease

7. How will an open-market sale of bonds by the Federal Reserve affect the inflation rate in the United States and the international value of the U.S. dollar?

	Inflation Rate	International Value of the U.S. Dollar
(A)	Increase	Depreciate
(B)	Increase	Appreciate
(C)	Decrease	Depreciate
(D)	Decrease	Appreciate
(E)	No change	No change

ANSWERS

Basic Economic Concepts

SCARCITY, CHOICE, AND OPPORTUNITY COSTS

DIFFICULTY LEVEL 1

1. CORRECT ANSWER: D

All resources are scarce, so individuals and societies are forced to make choices about how they utilize resources. Since resources are limited, we cannot fulfill an unlimited amount of demand for goods and services. For example, there is only so much fresh water available in a desert, so we cannot fulfill an unlimited demand there for agriculture or consumption.

INCORRECT ANSWER

All economies experience the limitations of scarcity. Scarcity forces societies to make some difficult choices about what to produce and what not to produce.

2. CORRECT ANSWER: B

Scarcity is present in every economy. There are limited resources and no economy can fulfill unlimited wants. Therefore, people are forced to make choices about how to utilize resources and what to produce.

INCORRECT ANSWER

While all of the choices present a problem, four of the five choices are problems that are not faced by *every* economy. The correct choice is the problem that underlies all of economics, forcing every society to make choices about what to produce.

3. CORRECT ANSWER: B

Scarcity is the most critical problem of economics. Because resources are scarce, or limited in supply, societies cannot produce an unlimited amount of goods and services. Scarcity forces economies to make choices about what will be produced and what will not be produced. These choices form the foundation of economic study.

Each choice presents a challenging problem for any economy, but the correct choice is the problem that underlies all of the other problems.

4. CORRECT ANSWER: A

When a decision is made, the next best alternative that was not chosen is the opportunity cost. For example, consider if you could purchase only one hat. Your favorite colors are blue and red. If you choose to buy a blue hat, it will cost you the opportunity to buy a red hat.

INCORRECT ANSWER

All of these terms are important basic economic concepts. Look for the term that signifies something given up or a chance that was not taken.

5. CORRECT ANSWER: C

The opportunity cost of Jiang's decision is the next best decision he did not make. If he were not bicycling, he'd be running, so running is his true opportunity cost. The key is to understand that Jiang would not be doing *all* of the other things if he were not bicycling.

INCORRECT ANSWER

When Jiang chooses to bicycle, what is he not choosing to do?

6. CORRECT ANSWER: D

Wheat is a land resource. It will be refined into a finished product such as bread or pizza. An oven is a physical capital resource. It will be utilized as a tool in producing a final product. A pizza is not a resource used to make something else. It is a final product that will be consumed.

INCORRECT ANSWER

A resource is used to make a final product. Which of these items will be used to make something else?

7. CORRECT ANSWER: B

A truck driver is a labor resource, but the training and knowledge the truck driver possesses is human capital. The more training, or human capital, the driver gains, the more productive the driver will become.

Basic Economic Concepts

INCORRECT ANSWER

It is important to distinguish between the various resources needed to perform the service of truck drivers. There's the truck itself, the gasoline, the driver, and the knowledge the driver possesses. How do you categorize the driver's safety training?

DIFFICULTY LEVEL 2

8. CORRECT ANSWER: D

Something is scarce when it is desired and limited. While air is not scarce, clean air is (particularly in a growing economy). Coal is also scarce. Since floppy disks are obsolete, we no longer desire them, so they are not scarce.

INCORRECT ANSWER

Remember, something is scarce when it is desired and limited. Which of this situations represents a resource or good that is *both* desired and limited?

9. CORRECT ANSWER: B

There is a limited supply of skilled computer programmers in the world and they are desired to perform the work needed to create computer applications. Since they are desired and limited, they are scarce.

INCORRECT ANSWER

Skilled computer programmers are a valuable resource for a company like Microsoft. Why might the company find it difficult to hire enough of them?

10. CORRECT ANSWER: A

The opportunity cost of a decision is the next best choice you would have made.

INCORRECT ANSWER

If you didn't choose chicken, you would have chosen one of the other options—which one?

11. CORRECT ANSWER: D

If there were unlimited resources then economies could produce unlimited goods at no cost. We would never need to make choices because we could have it all. If resources were not scarce, there would be no opportunity costs.

If you could have everything you wanted, would you need to make any choices?

PRODUCTION POSSIBILITIES CURVE

DIFFICULTY LEVEL 1

1. CORRECT ANSWER:E

When producing at an economy's maximum potential, it is impossible to produce more of one good without producing less of another.

INCORRECT ANSWER

If an economy is producing at peak efficiency, it is impossible to make some people better off without making others worse off. Considering this fact, what would happen if the economy tried to make book consumers better off?

DIFFICULTY LEVEL 2

2. CORRECT ANSWER: D

The production possibilities curve represents a level of production that utilizes an economy's resources to their fullest potential. Any production level that appears on the PPC indicates that no resources are left unused and there is no possible way to produce more efficiently.

INCORRECT ANSWER

Remember that it is impossible to produce at a level that is beyond "production possibilities". With that in mind, what does a point on the PPC represent?

3. CORRECT ANSWER: B

The production possibilities curve represents a level of production that utilizes an economy's resources to their fullest potential. Any production level that appears within the PPC indicates that some resources are left unused and that it is possible to produce more efficiently.

INCORRECT ANSWER

Remember that the PPC represents an economy's maximum possibilities. With that in mind, what does a point within the PPC represent?

4. **CORRECT ANSWER: C**

The PPC shifts outward when there is economic growth (i.e. an expansion of an economy's maximum possibilities). New technology is the only option that would improve upon these possibilities. A decrease in the unemployment rate seems tempting, but that would only bring an economy closer to the PPC, it would not cause an increase in maximum possibilities.

INCORRECT ANSWER

A shift of the PPC represents economic growth (i.e. an expansion of an economy's maximum possibilities). Be sure to distinguish between bringing an economy closer to what is possible and actually improving on what is possible.

5. **CORRECT ANSWER: E**

If one lawnmower is being produced, then there are 95 rakes being produced. If a second lawnmower is produced then only 85 rakes are being produced, a decrease of 10 rakes.

INCORRECT ANSWER

If one lawnmower is being produced, how many rakes are being produced? If two lawnmowers are being produced, what happens to the quantity of rakes that are produced?

6. **CORRECT ANSWER: D**

An inefficient level of production lies within the PPC. 70 rakes and 2 lawnmowers is the only combination that fulfills this criteria.

INCORRECT ANSWER

Where do the coordinates of rakes and lawnmowers need to lie on the graph in order to indicate a level of production that is inefficient?

7. **CORRECT ANSWER: E**

The graph indicates this economy's possibilities. It does not indicate what level of production the people in this economy prefer or need. Without further information about this economy, it is impossible to know whether more rakes or lawnmowers are needed.

INCORRECT ANSWER

The PPC tells us what an economy can produce. Does it tell us what an economy *should* produce?

8. **CORRECT ANSWER: E**

The opportunity cost is the number of units of a good that are lost when producing more of the other good. When you produce more sprockets you must give up some cogs, when you produce more cogs, you must give up some sprockets. The values on the graph indicate exactly how many of one good are given up when producing the other.

INCORRECT ANSWER

The options here ask you to consider the opportunity cost of moving from one point on the graph to another. When figuring out opportunity cost, you must calculate how much of a good is being lost to produce more of the other. For example, when you move from point X to point Z, you are producing more cogs but the opportunity cost is the number of sprockets you needed to give up (25). Use this same reasoning to determine if options II and III.

9. **CORRECT ANSWER: D**

Since Point F lies beyond the PPC, it lies beyond the economy's current maximum possibilities. This economy can only produce at Point F if it acquires more resources or improves its current resources in the future.

INCORRECT ANSWER

The PPC tells us the maximum level of production with current resources. What does it mean when a point lies beyond the line?

10. **CORRECT ANSWER: C**

If a point lies inside the PPC then it represents a level of production that is inefficient. This economy could produce more tractors *and* tomatoes if it used all of its resources efficiently.

INCORRECT ANSWER

Any combination of tractors and tomatoes that lies on the PPC can only be produced by using all available resources. So, to produce at a level that lies within the PPC, there must be resources that are not being used.

11. **CORRECT ANSWER: C**

If two tractors are being produced, then there are 80 tons of tomatoes being produced. If a third tractor is produced then only 55 tons of tomatoes are being produced, a decrease of 25 tons of tomatoes.

If one tractor is being produced, how many tons of tomatoes are being produced? If two tractors are being produced, what happens to the quantity of tomatoes that are produced?

DIFFICULTY LEVEL 3

12. CORRECT ANSWER: E

Effiency means that people cannot be made better off without making others worse off. If an economy is producing inefficiently then it could be making better use of resources so it can produce more of all goods without any opportunity cost.

If an economy is producing efficiently, there are resources that are not being fully utilized. If it were to fully utilize these resources, what would change?

COMPARATIVE ADVANTAGE, ABSOLUTE ADVANTAGE, SPECIALIZATION AND EXCHANGE

DIFFICULTY LEVEL 1

1. CORRECT ANSWER: D

Determining absolute advantage is simple—can one economy produce more of a good or service than another? If so, then it has an absolute advantage.

INCORRECT ANSWER

Be sure not to confuse absolute advantage and comparative advantage. Absolute advantage is simple—Which economy can produce more of a good or service?

DIFFICULTY LEVEL 2

2. CORRECT ANSWER: A

Comparative advantage means that in producing one of two products, an economy can produce a product at a lower opportunity cost than another economy.

INCORRECT ANSWER

Be sure not to confuse absolute advantage and comparative advantage. Also, you can certainly eliminate choice C since having an advantage implies that you produce something better, not equal to, another economy.

The following questions are based on the table below, which shows the production alternatives of two countries, Northland and Southland, producing two goods, cell phones and telelvisions, using all of their available resources.

3. CORRECT ANSWER: A

Right! Every time Northland produces a cell phone, it loses the opportunity to produce half of a television (20 televisions/40 cell phones). When Southland produces a cell phone, it loses the opportunity to produce 1 television (10 televisions/10 cell phones).

INCORRECT ANSWER

To determine the opportunity cost of producing 1 cell phone, use the "other output over" method. Since it's the opportunity cost of a cell phone you're looking for, take the other good, televisions, and put it over cell phones. So 1 cell phone costs televisions/cell phones.

4. **CORRECT ANSWER: D**

Right! Every time Northland produces a television, it loses the opportunity to produce 2 cell phones (40 cell phones/20 televisions). When Southland produces a television, it loses the opportunity to produce 1 cell phone (10 cell phones/10 televisions).

INCORRECT ANSWER

To determine the opportunity cost of producing 1 television, use the "other output over" method. Since it's the opportunity cost of a television you're looking for, take the other good, cell phones, and put it over televisions. So 1 television costs cell phones/televisions.

5. **CORRECT ANSWER: B**

Opportunity cost questions require that you are patient in figuring out the appropriate ratio. For Easton, one strawberry costs 20 radios/10 strawberries and for Weston, one strawberry costs 30 radios/30 strawberries.

INCORRECT ANSWER

Opportunity cost questions require that you are patient in figuring out the appropriate ratio. The graph shows the output possibilities for each economy, so you can use the "other output over" method. You are seeking the opportunity cost for a strawberry so in creating the ration put the other good, radios, over strawberries. For Easton, one strawberry costs 20 radios/10 strawberries and for Weston, one strawberry costs 30 radios/30 strawberries.

6. **CORRECT ANSWER: C**

Westland can outproduce Eastland (absolute advantage) and Easton has a lower opportunity cost in producing radios (comparative advantage).

INCORRECT ANSWER

Absolute advantage means an economy can outproduce another. Which economy can produce more radios? Which can produce more strawberries? Comparative advantage means an economy has a lower cost in producing a good. Which economy gives up fewer strawberries when producing a radio? Which gives up fewer radios when producing a unit of strawberries?

7. CORRECT ANSWER: B

An economy will only engage in trade for a good when the terms of trade offer it a lower cost when trading for the good than the cost if it were to produce the good itself.

INCORRECT ANSWER

If Eastland were to produce strawberries itself, it would give up 2 radios. Which terms of trade would provide it with a lower cost?

8. CORRECT ANSWER: A

Since the table provides the hours of labor needed to produce a unit of each good, we must use the input method of calculating opportunity cost. When figuring the opportunity cost of a lobster, the ratio should be lobsters/bananas.

INCORRECT ANSWER

To figure out the opportunity cost of producing one unit of lobster, create a ratio using lobster/bananas.

9. CORRECT ANSWER: D

Nation A has an absolute advantage in producing both goods because it can each good faster than Nation B.

Nation A has a comparative advantage only in the production of bananas because it can produce 1 banana at the opportunity cost of 2 lobster while Nation B produces 1 banana at the cost of 3 lobster.

When Nation A produces 1 lobster, it costs it ½ of a banana while Nation B can produce 1 lobster at the cost of only 1/3 of a banana.

Finally, when these two nations trade 2.5 units of lobster for 1 unit of bananas, it is mutually advantageous because it is less costly for each nation to trade at this cost than to produce each good itself.

INCORRECT ANSWER

A nation has an absolute advantage if it can produce a greater output than another nation. Who can produce more lobster in an hour? How about bananas?

A nation has a comparative advantage if it can produce one unit of a good at a lower cost than the other nation (in terms of the other good). When Nation A produces one lobster, how many bananas can it not produce? To figure out the math, just consider that for Nation A producing 1 lobster costs 10/20 bananas, or ½ of a banana.

Once you've calculated all of the opportunity costs, each nation should focus on producing the good in which it has a comparative advantage. The nations should then trade at a rate that would cost each nation less than if it were to produce the good itself.

DIFFICULTY LEVEL 3

10. CORRECT ANSWER: B

To gain from trade, a nation should specialize in production in which it has a comparative advantage and trade for a good in which another nation has a comparative advantage. In this case, Northland has a comparative advantage in cell phones and Southland has a comparative advantage in televisions.

INCORRECT ANSWER

There are a few steps for answering this question. First, determine the opportunity cost for each nation in producing a cell phone and a television. Then, determine which nation has the comparative advantage in producing each good. Northland should export the good in which it has a comparative advantage and import the good in which Southland has a comparative advantage.

The following questions are based on the diagram below, which shows the production alternatives of two countries, Easton and Westland, in producing two goods, strawberries and radios, using all of their available resources.

DEMAND, SUPPLY, AND MARKET EQUILIBRIUM

DIFFICULTY LEVEL 2

1. CORRECT ANSWER: C

The law of demand states that when the price of a good decreases, the quantity demanded of that good decreases. When the prices of cell phones decrease, consumers will demand a higher quantity.

INCORRECT ANSWER

Demand means that a consumer has the desire for a good and the ability to purchase it. The law of demand explains how consumers behave when price changes. Which choice best explains how consumers react to a changing price?

2. CORRECT ANSWER: B

Complementary goods are usually purchased together. If the price of one of these goods decreases then consumers will demand a higher quantity of that good. In addition, they will increase their demand for the other complementary good, regardless of its price. Some common examples of complementary goods are coffee and sugar, peanut butter and jelly, automobiles and gasoline.

INCORRECT ANSWER

Try looking at the situation in reverse. When the price of tea falls, how will consumers react? If consumers then demand more honey, what can we conclude about the relationship between honey and tea?

3. CORRECT ANSWER: A

If these goods are substitutes, then consumers are happy to consume either good and will simply demand whichever good is sold at the lower price. Therefore, if yams are rising in price, consumers are happy to purchase the relatively less expensive sweet potatoes.

INCORRECT ANSWER

If these goods are substitutes, then consumers are happy to consume either good and will simply demand whichever good is sold at the lower price.

4. **CORRECT ANSWER: B**

Any change that reduces the costs of production of a good will cause the supply of that good to increase. If cell phones can be produced more efficiently, then the supply of cell phones will increase.

INCORRECT ANSWER

When the costs of production change, supply changes. If the production of cell phones becomes more efficient, will the supply of cell phones increase or decrease?

5. **CORRECT ANSWER: C**

A leftward shift of the supply curve indicates that a cost of production is increasing. In this case, an increase in the cost of a productive input has caused the increase in cost of production.

INCORRECT ANSWER

A decrease (leftward shift) of supply results from the cost of production rising. Which answer choice indicates production costs rising?

6. **CORRECT ANSWER: E**

At a price of $7, the quantity supplied is 70 sandwiches while the quantity demanded is only 30 sandwiches, a surplus of 40 sandwiches.

INCORRECT ANSWER

At a market price of $7, what is the difference between the quantity supplied and the quantity demanded?

7. **CORRECT ANSWER: E**

A population increase causes an increase in demand (a rightward shift). Equilibrium price and quantity would increase. The equilibrium point would move upward and to the right *along* the supply curve, representing an increase in quantity supplied.

INCORRECT ANSWER

An increase in population causes an increase in demand, therefore demand will shift to the right. Trace the effects of this shift and test out each of the statements. Also, be mindful of the difference between a shift and a movement along the curve.

8. **CORRECT ANSWER: C**

If supply remains the same and demand increases, equilibrium price and quantity will necessarily increase. In answering these types of market questions, it is a good idea to draw a basic supply and demand graph and test your answer.

INCORRECT ANSWER

If you are having trouble arriving at an answer, it is a good idea to draw a basic supply and demand graph and test answers. Another consideration is that the question is asking what changes will "definitely" result in an increase in equilbrium price and quantity. This suggests that only one factor changes, supply or demand. Test those answers in your graph first.

MACROECONOMIC ISSUES: BUSINESS CYCLE, UNEMPLOYMENT, INFLATION, GROWTH

DIFFICULTY LEVEL 1

1. **CORRECT ANSWER: E**

   Falling output and employment are the required attributes of a recession.

   INCORRECT ANSWER

   While many factors can change in a recession, the required changes to make a recession occur in output and employment. How do they change?

2. **CORRECT ANSWER: A**

   When an economy is at its peak, the only way it can go is down. A recession always follows the peak.

   INCORRECT ANSWER

   When an economy is at its peak, the only way it can go is down. Eliminate any answer choices that suggest the economy continuing to improve.

3. **CORRECT ANSWER: B**

   Since Point A is a peak and Point B is a trough, the movement between must show a contraction of the economy.

   INCORRECT ANSWER

   Between Point A and Point B is a period in which Real GDP is decreasing. Which answer choice represents a period of declining output?

DIFFICULTY LEVEL 2

4. **CORRECT ANSWER: E**

   A business cycle is a pattern of expansion, contraction, and recovery in an economy. As the economy moves through this cycle, output and employment change.

INCORRECT ANSWER

There are a few answer choices that don't quite fit here. Productivity refers to the output of an individual unit of labor, which does not really explain expansion and contraction in the economy. Look for an answer that describes the general amount of activity occuring in an economy.

5. **CORRECT ANSWER: B**

While there are many changes that can occur during an economic expansion, it is certain that output will increase and unemployment will decrease.

INCORRECT ANSWER

During an economic expansion, output must be increasing—but that is not an answer choice. What other change must accompany an increase in output?

6. **CORRECT ANSWER: D**

A command economy is dictated by a central authority rather than by the free interaction of buyers and sellers in a market.

INCORRECT ANSWER

The opposite of a command economy is a market economy, in which buyers and sellers interact freely. Command economies are planned—but who does the planning?

DIFFICULTY LEVEL 3

7. **CORRECT ANSWER: D**

While unemployment and underutilization of resources are necessary characteristics of a recession, inflation is not. Inflation is present during a type of recession called stagflation, which is caused by a decrease in aggregate supply. However, it is possible to have inflation while an economy is expanding, so it is not necessarily a characteristic of a recession.

INCORRECT ANSWER

A recession is a downturn in output to a level that is below an economy's potential level of output. When output falls, what other characteristics are present? Now consider what problems emerge when an economy produces output beyond its potential output. What characteristics are present then?

Measurement of Economic Performance

NATIONAL INCOME ACCOUNTS

TOPIC 1: CIRCULAR FLOW

DIFFICULTY LEVEL 2

1. **CORRECT ANSWER: B**

   Households purchase needs and wants from firms and they sell factors of production to firms. For example, a household might buy food from a grocery store and a member of a household may sell his or her labor to a grocery store.

   INCORRECT ANSWER

   It may help to consider some examples of goods and services and factors of production. Consider food as a good and labor as a factor of production. Which does a household buy and which does it sell?

2. **CORRECT ANSWER: B**

   Households demand goods and services and supply factors of production such as labor and land.

   INCORRECT ANSWER

   Remember what is sold in the factor and product markets. Factor markets sell resources, such as labor. Product markets sell goods and services.

3. **CORRECT ANSWER: B**

   Savings do not represent income. Rather, savings represents the portion of income that a family does not spend or use to pay taxes.

INCORRECT ANSWER

Income represents the different manners in which a household can receive funds, not what a household may choose to do with its funds.

4. **CORRECT ANSWER: D**

In the diagram, the government is spending $200 on goods and services. The source of these funds is represented by the arrow pointing into the government, which shows that the government is receiving $200 from taxes.

INCORRECT ANSWER

To find the source of income for the government, look for any arrows pointing into government.

5. **CORRECT ANSWER: C**

There are two ways to measure GDP in this diagram. One way is to add up all of the spending according to the formula GDP = C + I + G + (X – Im). The other way is to add up all of the income: wages + profit/dividends + interest + rent. Either method will amount to $700.

INCORRECT ANSWER

There are two ways to measure GDP in this diagram. One way is to add up all of the spending according to the formula GDP = C + I + G + (X – Im). The other way is to add up all of the income: wages + profit/dividends + interest + rent.

6. **CORRECT ANSWER: B**

There are two ways to measure GDP in this diagram. One way is to add up all of the spending according to the formula GDP = C + I + G + (X – Im). The other way is to add up all of the income: wages + profit/dividends + interest + rent. Either method will amount to $800.

INCORRECT ANSWER

There are two ways to measure GDP in this diagram. One way is to add up all of the spending according to the formula GDP = C + I + G + (X – Im). The other way is to add up all of the income: wages + profit/dividends + interest + rent.

DIFFICULTY LEVEL 3

7. **CORRECT ANSWER: A**

The circular flow model traces spending. If spending is not occuring, then an agent in the model must be saving. Saving represents a leakage in the circular flow model.

INCORRECT ANSWER

The circular flow model traces spending. If spending is not occuring, then there is leakage from the circular flow model. If an agent in the model is not spending, what is it doing instead.

8. **CORRECT ANSWER: D**

For statements I and II you must remember that for each agent in a circular flow diagram, income equals expenditures. You can test that by adding up the value of any arrows pointing into an agent and ensuring the sum is equal to any arrows pointing out. For statement III, remember that net exports is equal to exports minus imports.

INCORRECT ANSWER

Same as above.

TOPIC 2: GDP

DIFFICULTY LEVEL 1

9. **CORRECT ANSWER: C**

Right! Gross domestic product is determined by adding together all of the spending on domestic production and subtracting imports, which represents spending on foreign production.

INCORRECT ANSWER

Gross domestic product is determined by adding together all of the spending on domestic production and subtracting any spending on foreign production.

10. CORRECT ANSWER: B

There are two ways to measure GDP in this table. One way is to add up all of the spending according to the formula GDP = C + I + G + (X – Im). The other way is to add up all of the income: wages + profit/dividends + interest + rent. Be sure to exclude transfers (unemployment benefits) and taxes (sales tax) when calculating.

INCORRECT ANSWER

There are two ways to measure GDP in this table. One way is to add up all of the spending according to the formula GDP = C + I + G + (X – Im). The other way is to add up all of the income: wages + profit/dividends + interest + rent. Be sure to exclude any superfluous data that has been included in the table to throw you off.

11. CORRECT ANSWER: A

GDP = wages + profits + interest + rent. Plug in the given data and do your math!

INCORRECT ANSWER

Same as above.

12. CORRECT ANSWER: E

When calculating government spending one must account for the total spending of all government, whether local, state, or national government. In this case, the local government has spent $300 and the Federal government has spent $200, for a total of $500 in government spending.

INCORRECT ANSWER

Have you included the spending from all parts of government?

13. CORRECT ANSWER: B

Net exports equal exports minus imports. Exports are included in a nation's GDP because they represent spending on domestic production. Imports are excluded because they represent spending on a different nation's production.

INCORRECT ANSWER

Remember to include exports in GDP, but to exclude imports.

14. CORRECT ANSWER: C

GDP includes consumption spending ($600), investment spending ($300), all government spending ($500), and exports ($20). Imports ($40) are subtracted from GDP.

INCORRECT ANSWER

Remember the formula for GDP. $GDP = C + I + G + (X - Im)$

DIFFICULTY LEVEL 3

15. CORRECT ANSWER: B

Each agent in this process is adding some value to the cucumbers to make them into a final product—pickles. When deciding what value to include in GDP, it is important not to double-count any value added. The simplest way to do this is to include the final sale price to the customer in GDP, which is the $3 sale price from the grocery store to the final customer. That $3 includes all of the value added to the pickles along its way from farm to customer.

INCORRECT ANSWER

Each agent in this process is adding some value to the cucumbers to make them into a final product—pickles. When deciding what value to include in GDP, it is important not to double-count any value added.

TOPIC 3: COMPONENTS OF GROSS DOMESTIC PRODUCT

DIFFICULTY LEVEL 2

16. CORRECT ANSWER: C

Each choice concerns the purchase of a computer, but to be included in this year's GDP as consumption spending it must be produced in the U.S., purchased new, by a private individual, and for private use. Choice C is the only response that fits these criteria.

INCORRECT ANSWER

Each choice concerns the purchase of a computer, but to be included in this year's GDP as consumption spending it must be produced in the U.S., purchased new, by a private individual, and for private use.

17. CORRECT ANSWER: E

Investment spending includes spending on final goods and/or services that are used to produce other goods and services, spending on the construction of new properties, or additions to a business' inventory. Investment spending *does not* include the purchase of financial assets, like stocks and bonds.

INCORRECT ANSWER

Same as above.

18. CORRECT ANSWER: D

Used goods are excluded from this year's GDP because they were already counted in GDP in the year they were produced.

INCORRECT ANSWER

Consider what goods are included in this year's GDP: final products that are produced within the economy this year. One of the choices does not meet these criteria.

19. CORRECT ANSWER: A

When a private individual purchases a final good or service it is considered consumption spending. Were the lawn mower purchased by a landscaping company then it would have been categorized as investment spending.

INCORRECT ANSWER

A private individual is purchasing the lawn mower, not a firm, such as a landscaping company.

20. CORRECT ANSWER: D

Any increase in consumption spending, investment spending, government spending, or spending on exports, or a decrease in spending on imports, will increase a nation's GDP. In addition, the spending must be for new, final products produced within the domestic economy. The government purchase of new computer equipment is the only choice that fits these criteria.

INCORRECT ANSWER

Any increase in consumption spending, investment spending, government spending, or spending on exports, or a decrease in spending on imports, will increase a nation's GDP. In addition, the spending must be for new, final products produced within the domestic economy.

21. CORRECT ANSWER: B

Used goods are not included in GDP because they were counted in GDP in the year they were produced. Consider if the antique desk was first sold in 1925 for $20, then it was counted as $20 in 1925's GDP.

The other choices are included in 2000's GDP. Rent is considered payment for a service, a new sofa is considered consumption spending, commissions are considered payment to the salesperson for his or her services, and the automobiles would count as the U.S.'s GDP because the production is located within the U.S.

INCORRECT ANSWER

Some questions to consider when choosing your answer: Does the answer choice represent the purchase of a final good or service? Is the purchase for a new good? Does the answer represent production that took place in 2000? Does the answer represent production that took place within the U.S.?

DIFFICULTY LEVEL 3

22. CORRECT ANSWER: B

Gross domestic product represents production, not sales. If an automobile is produced in 2013, then it is counted in 2013's GDP. Since it did not sell in 2013, it cannot be considered consumption spending. Rather, it is included as investment spending in 2013—it is an addition to inventory.

INCORRECT ANSWER

Gross domestic product represents production, not sales. If an automobile is produced in 2013, then it is counted in 2013's GDP. However, since it did not sell in 2013, it cannot be considered consumption spending. What type of spending does it represent?

TOPIC 4: REAL VERSUS NOMINAL GROSS DOMESTIC PRODUCT

DIFFICULTY LEVEL 1

23. CORRECT ANSWER: C

Real GDP measures the actual output of an economy adjusted for changes in price level.

INCORRECT ANSWER

Remember that GDP is a measurement of production that considers the quantity of the goods and services produced and the value of those goods and services. What factor can influence the value of production?

24. **CORRECT ANSWER: B**

Nominal GDP is determined by adding up the value of all production in a given year. To do this calculation, multiply the quantity of each good by its price in that year to get the value and then add together all of the values.

INCORRECT ANSWER

Same as above.

DIFFICULTY LEVEL 2

25. **CORRECT ANSWER: C**

To determine Real GDP for the year 2000, multiply 2000 quantities by the base year's (1999) prices.

INCORRECT ANSWER

Same as above.

DIFFICULTY LEVEL 3

26. **CORRECT ANSWER: A**

Real GDP is nominal GDP controlled for inflation. If real GDP is rising, then we can safely conclude that output is increasing. If nominal GDP is rising at a faster rate than real GDP, then we must also conclude that the price level is rising.

INCORRECT ANSWER

Real GDP is nominal GDP controlled for inflation. If real GDP is rising, then we can safely conclude that output is increasing. If output is increasing, then the economy cannot be experiencing a recession. What does it mean that nominal GDP is growing at a faster rate than real GDP?

27. CORRECT ANSWER: C

The formula for calculating the GDP deflator is (Nominal GDP/Real GDP) x 100.

Incorrect answer: Same as above

28. CORRECT ANSWER: A

The only way that nominal GDP can increase is if price level rises, output quantity increases, or both. The answer that includes all of these possibilities is choice A. Choice C is tempting but *both* do not have to occur for nominal GDP to increase.

INCORRECT ANSWER

Consider which answer choice has elements that are *necessary* for nominal GDP to increase. There is one incorrect answer choice that can cause nominal GDP to increase, but it fails to include other possible causes for nominal GDP to increase.

INFLATION MEASUREMENT AND ADJUSTMENT

TOPIC 1: PRICE INDICES

DIFFICULTY LEVEL 1

1. CORRECT ANSWER: C

The consumer price index measures the prices of about 80,000 goods and services typically consumed by urban families. This is the main measurement of inflation in the United States.

INCORRECT ANSWER

When measuring inflation, it would be impractical to include the price of all goods and services produced in the economy. What type of products does the CPI sample?

DIFFICULTY LEVEL 2

2. CORRECT ANSWER: C

The total price of a market basket containing these goods costs $100 in 1999 and $110 in 200. The price level increased by 10%.

INCORRECT ANSWER

The quantity does not change from 1999 to 2000, but prices do. If one were to purchase those quantities at 1999 prices, how much would it total? How much would it total in 2000? What is the percent difference between 1999 and 2000?

3. CORRECT ANSWER: A

The price index of the base year is 100—always.

Incorrect answer: Nothing too fancy is needed here—the price index is always the same number, no matter what the price of the market basket.

4. **CORRECT ANSWER: B**

To determine the price index for Year 2, divide ($220/$200) X 100. Another way to think of this problem is to consider that $220 is 10% greater than $200. Since the index in the base year is 100, the index in Year 2 must be an index that is 10% greater than 100.

INCORRECT ANSWER

There is a formula for determining the price index of a particular year: (Basket price of current year / Basket price of base year) X 100. Plug in the provided numbers and do the math!

5. **CORRECT ANSWER: A**

To determine the price index for Year 1, divide ($180/$240) X 100. Another way to think of this problem is to consider that $180 is 25% less than than $240. Since the index in the base year is 100, the index in Year 2 must be an index that is 25% less than 100.

INCORRECT ANSWER

The interesting part of this problem is that the market basket in Year 1 costs less than it does in Year 2, but Year 2 is the base year. Since the base year's index must be 100, then the index for Year 1 will be a number less than 100. How much less than 100?

6. **CORRECT ANSWER: A**

The rate of inflation between two periods of time is determined by the following formula:

$$Inflation\ rate = \frac{CPI2 - CPI1}{CPI1} \times 100$$

In this case, the inflation rate works out to be 10 percent. Another way to consider this problem is that the index 110 is 10% greater than the index 100.

INCORRECT ANSWER

The rate of inflation between two periods of time is determined by the following formula:

$$Inflation\ rate = \frac{CPI2 - CPI1}{CPI1} \times 100$$

7. **CORRECT ANSWER: B**

The rate of inflation between two periods of time is determined by the following formula:

193

$$Inflation\ rate = \frac{CPI2 - CPI1}{CPI1} \times 100$$

In this case, the inflation rate works out to be 25 percent. Another way to consider this problem is that the index 150 is 25% greater than the index 125.

INCORRECT ANSWER

The rate of inflation between two periods of time is determined by the following formula:

$$Inflation\ rate = \frac{CPI2 - CPI1}{CPI1} \times 100$$

8. **CORRECT ANSWER: D**

The consumer price index measures the prices of a market basket of selected goods and services purchased by the average consumer. If the CPI doubles, then the value of this market basket must have doubled.

INCORRECT ANSWER

It is clear that the consumer price index has doubled. What exactly does the CPI measure?

9. **CORRECT ANSWER: E**

The GDP deflator is found by taking the total price of a basket of goods in one period and dividing it by the total price of the same basket of goods in another period and multiplying the result by 100.

INCORRECT ANSWER

Same as above.

10. **CORRECT ANSWER: C**

To determine the GDP deflator, divide nominal GDP by real GDP and then multiply the result by 100. The result is 125. Another idea to consider is that since real GDP is less than nominal GDP, then there must have been an increase in price level to account for the $20 billion difference between nominal and real GDP. To account for that 25% difference in GDP, prices must have increased by 25%.

Since real GDP is less than nominal GDP, there must have been an increase in price level. Therefore, the GDP deflator must be greater than 100. How much inflation occurred?

TOPIC 2: NOMINAL AND REAL VALUES

DIFFICULTY LEVEL 2

11. CORRECT ANSWER: D

When there is unexpected inflation, borrowers benefit and lenders lose. In this case, the borrower will repay the loan with money that is less valuable than was originally anticipated. The lender hoped to earn 2 percent in real interest and 2 percent for expected inflation (for a total nominal interest rate of 4 percent). Due to unexpected inflation, the lender will still receive 4 percent nominal interest, but 3 percent is accounted for by actual inflation and only 1 percent from real interest.

Remember that the nominal interest rate is equal to the real interest rate plus expected inflation. If actual inflation turns out to be greater than expected, but nominal interest remains fixed, what will the lender really earn in interest?

12. CORRECT ANSWER: C

The real interest rate is equal to the nominal interest rate minus the inflation rate. In this case, the real interest rate equals 8 percent minus 3 percent.

Consider what information has been provided. The interest rate that banks charge customers is the nominal interest rate, which is 8%. The inflation rate is 3%. So how much interest is the bank really earning each year?

13. CORRECT ANSWER: B

When the actual rate of inflation is less than expected, those who borrowed money at the nominal rate would lose because they will be repaying their loans with money that is more valuable than they had expected. The real interest rate payed by the borrower would be larger than expected.

INCORRECT ANSWER

Remember that the nominal interest rate is equal to the real interest rate plus expected inflation. If actual inflation turns out to be less than expected, but the nominal interest rate remains fixed, what will the lender really earn in interest? Are these real interest earnings greater or less than the borrower expected?

14. CORRECT ANSWER: D

The real interest rate is equal to the nominal interest rate minus the expected inflation rate. The real interest rate is what the bank earns on a loan when controlling for the effects of inflation. The nominal interest rate is the rate at which the bank issues the loan to the borrower.

INCORRECT ANSWER

Be sure to understand the given information. The bank expects inflation to be 3% and issues the loan at 7%, which is the nominal interest rate. These rates can be used to determine the real interest rate.

15. CORRECT ANSWER: C

Borrowers benefit from unanticipated inflation because they are able to pay off their debts in dollars that are worth less purchasing power. However, this benefit is only realized if the borrower is repaying a fixed-rate loan. If the borrower is repaying a variable rate loan, then this benefit is indeterminate.

INCORRECT ANSWER

Inflation causes money to have less purchasing power. Who would benefit from a loan that is repayed with money that is less valuable—borrowers or lenders?

DIFFICULTY LEVEL 3

16. CORRECT ANSWER: C

The nominal interest rate is equal to the real interest rate plus the expected rate of inflation. In this case, the highest real interest rate Rafael will allow is 4 percent. Add 4 percent to the 6 percent inflation expectation to get the highest possible nominal rate Rafael will allow: 10 percent.

INCORRECT ANSWER

Consider the given information: expected inflation is 6 percent and real interest rate cannot exceed 4 percent. What is the highest interest rate a bank can charge Rafael?

TOPIC 3: COSTS OF INFLATION

DIFFICULTY LEVEL 2

17. CORRECT ANSWER: B

A shoe leather cost refers to the additional time that must be spent searching for lower prices, spending money before prices rise, and converting money to non-money assets. Shirley must frequently visit her bank to convert her money to an asset that retains value, which costs her time and effort.

INCORRECT ANSWER

Which term refers to the time and effort needed to reduce Shirley's money holdings?

18. CORRECT ANSWER: A

A shoe leather cost refers to the additional time that must be spent searching for lower prices, spending money before prices rise, and converting money to non-money assets. If inflation is reducing the purchasing power of money, an individual can now convert money to interest-bearing assets more easily by using a computer.

INCORRECT ANSWER

Technology has made it easier to conduct banking transactions from home, thus reducing the time and effort needed to travel to a bank and conduct transactions in person. Which term refers to thte time and effort needed to conduct transactions?

19. CORRECT ANSWER: B

Menu costs refer to the cost of updating prices amidst frequent price increases. Robert must pay additional staff to keep his prices updated, which is a cost he would not bear if prices were not rising.

INCORRECT ANSWER

Imagine a restaurant that must keep re-printing its menu frequently because prices keep rising. Which answer choice seems similar to this situation?

20. CORRECT ANSWER: D

Unit-of-account costs are experienced when people grow confused or unsure about the relative value of goods and services because rising prices have made money a less reliable measurement of value.

INCORRECT ANSWER

Prices are used to account for how valuable goods and services are. If prices rise often, how reliable is this measurement?

21. **CORRECT ANSWER: B**

Inflation erodes the purchasing power of a person's income. Tonya's nominal wages have increased by 5% but inflation has eroded the purchasing power of her wages by 3%, which means that her wage has really increased by only 2%-- her real wage increase.

INCORRECT ANSWER

Inflation erodes the purchasing power of a person's income. Tonya's nominal wages have increased by 5%, but how much of her purchasing power has been eroded? What does her wage increase really amount to?

UNEMPLOYMENT

TOPIC 1: DEFINITION AND MEASUREMENT

DIFFICULTY LEVEL 1

1. **CORRECT ANSWER: D**

   The labor force represents the people in an economy who are working or willing to work.

   INCORRECT ANSWER

   Working people are a part of the labor force. What other group should also be included?

DIFFICULTY LEVEL 2

2. **CORRECT ANSWER: B**

   Madison is willing and able to work and is actively seeking a job, so she is unemployed. The other choices represent individuals who are either employed or not a part of the labor force. A common incorrect choice is Julie, who has given up looking for work. Since she is no longer seeking a job, she is no longer a part of the labor force.

   INCORRECT ANSWER

   To be categorized as unemployed, a person must be willing and able to work and must be actively seeking a job. Put each choice through these criteria to find the answer.

3. **CORRECT ANSWER: E**

   If people are not working but are seeking employment, then they are unemployed. The cause of a person losing a previous job is irrelevant.

   INCORRECT ANSWER

   There are some tempting incorrect choices here. Keep in mind that to be classified as unemployed, one must not currently be working for pay and must be actively seeking a paying job.

4. **CORRECT ANSWER: C**

To measure the unemployment rate, use the following formula:

$$Unemployment\ rate\ = \frac{Number\ of\ people\ unemployed}{Number\ of\ people\ in\ the\ labor\ force} \times 100$$

In this case, there are 7 million people unemployed and 100 million people in the labor force, which amounts to an unemployment rate of 7.0%.

INCORRECT ANSWER

To measure the unemployment rate, use the following formula:

$$Unemployment\ rate\ = \frac{Number\ of\ people\ unemployed}{Number\ of\ people\ in\ the\ labor\ force} \times 100$$

Remember, the labor force is composed of the employed and the unemployed.

5. **CORRECT ANSWER: B**

To measure the unemployment rate, use the following formula:

$$Unemployment\ rate\ = \frac{Number\ of\ people\ unemployed}{Number\ of\ people\ in\ the\ labor\ force} \times 100$$

In this case, there are 5 million people unemployed and 100 million people in the labor force, which amounts to an unemployment rate of 5.0%. Be wary of superfluous information, such as the number of discouraged or retired workers.

INCORRECT ANSWER

To measure the unemployment rate, use the following formula:

$$Unemployment\ rate\ = \frac{Number\ of\ people\ unemployed}{Number\ of\ people\ in\ the\ labor\ force} \times 100$$

Remember, the labor force is composed of the employed and the unemployed. Be wary of superflous information, such as the number of discouraged or retired workers.

DIFFICULTY LEVEL 3

6. **CORRECT ANSWER: D**

Underemployed workers are being paid for part-time work, but they would prefer to work full-time. Regardless of their dissatisfaction with their employment situation, underemployed workers are counted as employed in the official unemployment rate.

INCORRECT ANSWER

In answering this question, first make sure the answer choice is accurate and then make sure that the choice represents a factor that would understate the true state of unemployment in the economy. The correct choice likely includes a class of workers who are employed, but dissatisfied with their employment situation.

TOPIC 2: TYPES OF UNEMPLOYMENT

DIFFICULTY LEVEL 1

7. CORRECT ANSWER: A

Cyclical unemployment is caused by downturns in the economy. When a recession occurs, output declines and producers often lay off workers, causing cyclical unemployment.

INCORRECT ANSWER

A recession is a part of the business cycle. What type of unemployment occurs in a downturn of the business cycle?

DIFFICULTY LEVEL 2

8. CORRECT ANSWER: B

Frictional unemployment is caused by the time it takes for job seekers and potential employers to find each other. If these websites become more popular, then this type of unemployment will be diminished.

INCORRECT ANSWER

What type of unemployment is caused by the difficulty in job seekers and potential employers finding one another?

9. CORRECT ANSWER: D

Structural unemployment results from improvements in technology or global changes in an industry that render a type of job unnecessary. When warehouse workers are structurally unemployed when their jobs are no longer needed because they have been replaced by computers.

INCORRECT ANSWER

Structural unemployment occurs when technology renders a job obselete or global changes in an industry enable the labor to be produced by workers in another economy. Which example fits one of these criteria?

10. CORRECT ANSWER: E

Structural unemployment results from improvements in technology or global changes in an industry that render a type of job unnecessary. When warehouse workers are structurally unemployed when their jobs are no longer needed because they have been replaced by computers.

INCORRECT ANSWER

Structural unemployment occurs when technology renders a job obselete or global changes in an industry enable the labor to be produced by workers in another economy. Which example fits one of these criteria?

11. CORRECT ANSWER: A

Frictional unemployment occurs during the period in between one job and another. Frictional unemployment occurs because workers and firms for which they are a good fit take time to find one another.

INCORRECT ANSWER

Vanessa voluntarily quit her job and is taking the time to find a new job that is the right fit. What type of unemployment best represents this situation?

TOPIC 3: NATURAL RATE OF UNEMPLOYMENT

DIFFICULTY LEVEL 2

12. CORRECT ANSWER: C

The natural rate of unemployment is equal to the sum of structural and frictional unemployment. An economy has achieved the natural rate of unemployment when it has eliminated cyclical unemployment.

INCORRECT ANSWER

Natural unemployment includes the categories of unemployment that occur at any point in the business cycle, whether the economy is experiencing an expansion or recession.

13. **CORRECT ANSWER: D**

An economy is said to be at full unemployment when it is measured at the natural rate of unemployment. The natural rate includes only frictional and structural unemployment.

INCORRECT ANSWER

Even during an economic expansion, there is still unemployment. If an economy is not in a recession, what types of unemployment remain?

14. **CORRECT ANSWER: B**

When an economy's actual rate of unemployment is equal to the natural rate of unemployment, it is producing at the long-run potential output level. There is no cyclical unemployment when the economy is at the natural rate of unemployment. If the actual rate increases beyond the natural rate, it is due to a downturn in the business cycle.

INCORRECT ANSWER

What categories of unemployment naturally occur in an economy at any point in the business cycle? What category of unemployment varies based on the business cycle?

15. **CORRECT ANSWER: C**

The actual rate of unemployment is equal to the natural rate plus the cyclical rate. If you subtract the natural rate of unemployment (5%) from the actual rate of unemployment (7%), you will find the cyclical rate of unemployment must be 2%.

INCORRECT ANSWER

Remember that the natural rate of unemployment is comprised of frictional and structural unemployment. If the actual rate is 7% and the natural rate is 5%, what type of unemployment comprises the remaining 2%?

DIFFICULTY LEVEL 3

16. CORRECT ANSWER: A

Increasing unemployment benefits would enable frictionally unemployed workers to spend more time seeking a job that best fits their skills. An increase in frictional unemployment would cause the natural rate of unemployment to increase.

INCORRECT ANSWER

Remember that the natural rate of unemployment includes frictional and structural unemployment. Any factor that increases one or both of these types of unemployment will alson increase natural unemployment.

National Income and Price Determination

AGGREGATE DEMAND

TOPIC 1: DETERMINANTS OF AGGREGATE DEMAND

DIFFICULTY LEVEL 2

1.   CORRECT ANSWER: C

There is an inverse relationship between price level and quantity of aggregate output demanded. As price level rises, the purchasing power of wealth like assets and savings falls. Also, interest rates rise so interest-sensitive spending falls. Finally, at higher prices, domestic exports decrease. Overall, the quantity of domestic output demanded decreases, which is represented by a movement upward and along the aggregate demand curve.

INCORRECT ANSWER

The answer choices reference the aggregate demand curve, which shows the relationship between price level and aggregate output demanded. The aggregate demand curve shows an inverse relationship between price level and quantity of aggregate output demanded. Try drawing the graph for help.

2.   CORRECT ANSWER: B

As price level rises, the purchasing power of wealth (assets and savings) falls. Since this wealth now has less purchasing power, consumer spending decreases.

INCORRECT ANSWER

Wealth include a household's assets and savings. What happens to the purchasing power of wealth as prices rise?

3. **CORRECT ANSWER: D**

Banks respond to a decrease in price level by decreasing interest rates. Interest-sensitive spending, such as auto, home, and physical capital purchases increase in response.

INCORRECT ANSWER

Among the prices that tend to decrease when price level falls is the price of a loan—the interest rate. How does a decrease in the interest rate affect interest-sensitive spending?

4. **CORRECT ANSWER: C**

To measure aggregate demand, add together all of the spending on domestic production: consumption spending, investment spending, government spending, and exports, and then subtract spending on imports.

INCORRECT ANSWER

To measure aggregate demand, add together all spending on domestic production and subtract domestic spending on foreign production.

5. **CORRECT ANSWER: E**

If changes in the stock market cause consumers' wealth to increase, consumers feel richer and tend to consume more.

INCORRECT ANSWER

Which change would make consumers feel richer?

6. **CORRECT ANSWER: B**

The graph shows a rightward shift of the aggregate demand curve, which indicates that aggregate demand is increasing at all price levels. The only choice that causes an increase in aggregate demand is an increase in consumer optimism.

Be careful not to select E, which would cause an increase in the quantity of aggregate output demanded. Such an increase would be represented by a movement downward along the AD1 curve.

7. **CORRECT ANSWER: E**

The movement from Point A to Point C represents an increase in aggregate demand, which can be caused by an increase in government expenditures. The other choices represent movements along the curve (caused by a change in price level) or a decrease in aggregate demand.

INCORRECT ANSWER

The movement from Point A to Point C represents an increase in aggregate demand, which cannot be caused by a price change. Eliminate those answer choices.

8. **CORRECT ANSWER: E**

The only choice that demonstrates a decrease in price level is a movement from Point A to Point B, which is a movement down along the curve. As the price falls, the value of consumers' wealth grows and they increase the quantity of aggregate output demanded.

INCORRECT ANSWER

When price level changes, there is a movement along the AD curve. When a factor other than price level changes, the AD curve shifts.

DIFFICULTY LEVEL 3

9. **CORRECT ANSWER: D**

A decrease in imports would increase the value of net exports. Net exports measures the total income earned from the sale of exports to foreigners minus the toal amount spent by a nation on goods and services imported from other countries. Net exports are a component of aggregate demand.

When answering this question, be sure to first eliminate the answer choices that reflect an influence on aggregate supply, such as labor productivity.

INCORRECT ANSWER

First, eliminate any answer choices that only influence aggregate supply. Secondly, remember that each factor is decreasing. For most factors that affect aggregate demand, a decrease would cause a decrease in aggregate demand. Which answer choice has the opposite effect?

10. **CORRECT ANSWER: B**

An increase in interest rates due to crowding out will cause private investment spending to decrease, which is represented by a shift to the left of the aggregate demand curve.

INCORRECT ANSWER

When interest rates rise, private investment spending decreases. Which movement demonstrates the effect on aggregate demand?

TOPIC 2: MULTIPLIER AND CROWDING-OUT EFFECTS

DIFFICULTY LEVEL 2

11. CORRECT ANSWER: A

When receiving a dollar of additional income, a person has two options: spend or save. The marginal propensity to save plus the marginal propensity to consume equals

Incorrect Answer

The marginal propensity to save plus the marginal propensity to consume equals 1.

12. CORRECT ANSWER: C

Use the formula for the multiplier:

$$Multiplier = \frac{1}{1 - MPC}$$

INCORRECT ANSWER

Use the formula for the multiplier:

$$Multiplier = \frac{1}{1 - MPC}$$

13. CORRECT ANSWER: A

When additional income is earned it can either be used for consumption or saving. If it is more likely that the income will be consumed, then it is necessarily less likely to be saved.

INCORRECT ANSWER

When choosing your answer, consider this concept: MPC + MPS = 1.

14. CORRECT ANSWER: A

If the marginal propensity to save is decreasing, then the marginal propensity to consume must be increasing. The more likely consumers are to spend than save, the larger the value of the multiplier. You can also consider the formula for determining the multiplier, in which the MPS is the denominator:

$$Multiplier = \frac{1}{MPS}$$

As the MPS decreases, the multiplier becomes a larger number.

INCORRECT ANSWER

Consider the formulae for determining the multiplier:

$$Multiplier = \frac{1}{1 - MPC}$$ Alternatively: $$Multiplier = \frac{1}{MPS}$$

When the denominator becomes a smaller number, the multiplier becomes a larger number.

15. **CORRECT ANSWER: C**

Since Terry's marginal propensity to consume is 0.8, his consumption spending will increase by a factor of 0.8 x additional income. Since he is earning $10,000 more this year, his additional spending is equal to 0.8 x $10,000, or $8,000.

Be sure to ignore the fact that he spent $45,000 of $50,000 last year. The MPC is the number used to determine how much of his *additional* income will be spent.

INCORRECT ANSWER

Be careful to disregard any superfluous information, such as how much Terry spent last year. You are tasked with determining how much *additional* spending he did *this* year. How much more money did he earn? How much of this additional income will he spend?

16. **CORRECT ANSWER: D**

When governments spending increases by $50 billion, the ultimate increase in output will be greater than this initial government expenditure. By using the MPC of 0.8 we can determine that the government spending multiplier is Multiply the $50 billion in government expenditures by 5 to get the maximum possible increase in output-- $250 billion.

INCORRECT ANSWER

When governments spending increases by $50 billion, the ultimate increase in output will be greater than this initial government expenditure. Use the marginal propensity to consume to help determine how much the initial $50 billion expenditure will continue to circulate in the economy.

17. **CORRECT ANSWER: D**

The marginal propensity to consume is used to determine the spending multiplier. The larger the MPC, the larger the spending multiplier.

Choice B is a tempting answer, but marginal propensity to consume is not equal to the percentage of *total* income spent on consumption. Rather, MPC is the ratio of a particular change in income spent on consumption.

INCORRECT ANSWER

The marginal propensity to consume is the ratio of a particular change in income spent on consumption. If a person with an MPC of 0.8 receives one dollar of additional income, that person will spend 80 cents of that dollar.

DIFFICULTY LEVEL 3

18. CORRECT ANSWER: D

If disposable income increases by $1100, then this is the amount multiplied by the marginal propensity to consume in order to determine how spending will increase. In this case, $1100 x 0.75 equals $825 of additional consumption spending.

INCORRECT ANSWER

The data to determine the correct answer has been provided to you, but be sure to disregard any unneeded information, such as the amount of autonomous consumption.

19. CORRECT ANSWER: E

Each of these choices will increase aggregate demand, but a decrease in taxes will have the smallest expansionary effect because people will not necessarily spend the entire $200 in additional income provided by the tax relief. In each of the other choices, the entire $200 is directly spent in the domestic economy.

INCORRECT ANSWER

Each of these choices will increase aggregate demand, but one of them will not cause consumption to multiply by as large of an amount.

20. CORRECT ANSWER: E

If the marginal propensity to consume is 0.75, then use the formula

$$Multiplier = \frac{1}{1 - MPC}$$) to determine the spending multiplier (4). Use this multiplier to determine the change in income that would result from one dollar of spending.

It is important to calculate the spending multiplier to determine the change in income that would result from one dollar of spending.

National Income and Price Determination

AGGREGATE SUPPLY

TOPIC 1: SHORT-RUN AND LONG-RUN ANALYSES

DIFFICULTY LEVEL 1

1. CORRECT ANSWER: A

The aggregate supply curve represents the changes in the quantity of aggregate output supplied at various price levels in an economy.

INCORRECT ANSWER

When drawing an aggregate supply curve, what labels are used on the axes?

2. CORRECT ANSWER: D

The short-run aggregate supply curve is positively sloped, indicating that as price level rises, the quantity of aggregate supply increases. This change is represented by an upward movement along the curve.

A common incorrect answer is that aggregate supply increases. An increase in aggregate supply indicates that the aggregate supply has increased at all price levels, which would be represented by a rightward shift of the SRAS curve.

INCORRECT ANSWER

The short-run aggregate supply curve is positively sloped. Try drawing the graph to determine the answer.

DIFFICULTY LEVEL 2

3. CORRECT ANSWER: D

It is assumed that wages and input prices are fixed, or "sticky," in the short-run and are flexible in the long-run.

INCORRECT ANSWER

The length of the short-run is not determined by a calendar, but rather by a change in the economy.

4. **CORRECT ANSWER: B**

The long-run aggregate supply curve is vertical because when labor prices are flexible, there is a quantity of output an economy that will produce that is independent of price level.

INCORRECT ANSWER

If the price of labor is flexible, then costs and profits for producers remain the same. Producers, therefore, have no incentive to produce more or less at different price levels. How is this situation represented in the AD-AS model?

5. **CORRECT ANSWER: A**

If input prices do not change and price level increases, then a producer is likely to be earning more profit per unit of production, as profit per unit equals price per unit minus cost per unit. As profits increase, producers have an incentive to increase production.

INCORRECT ANSWER

If input prices do not change but price level increases, profits rise for producers. How will producers respond to increasing profits?

DIFFICULTY LEVEL 3

6. **CORRECT ANSWER: B**

In the short-run, an increase in price level will cause aggregate output to increase because wages and input costs are sticky, and producers will earn more profit as prices rise. In the long-run, as wages adjust to rising prices, aggregate output will ultimately be unchanged.

INCORRECT ANSWER

Try drawing the short-run and long-run aggregate supply curves. Remember to label the axes correctly: price level is on the vertical axis and aggregate output is on the horizontal axis.

TOPIC 2: STICKY VERSUS FLEXIBLE WAGES AND PRICES

DIFFICULTY LEVEL 1

7. CORRECT ANSWER: D

Since wages are slow to change in the face of short-term economic fluctuations, economists refer to them as "sticky".

INCORRECT ANSWER

According to the description, wages do not immediately change in the face of short-term economic fluctuations. What term best fits this phenomenon?

DIFFICULTY LEVEL 2

8. CORRECT ANSWER: B

In the short-run, wages are fixed because labor contracts take time to renegotiate and workers will not readily accept immediate wage cuts in an economic downturn, nor will firms readily award higher wages if demand increases. In the long-run, there is time for these adjustments to take place.

INCORRECT ANSWER

Consider the conditions in the labor market. Many workers have contracts that are not easily changed in the face of a sudden change in economic conditions. Contracts take time to renegotiate.

TOPIC 3: DETERMINANTS OF AGGREGATE SUPPLY

DIFFICULTY LEVEL 2

9. CORRECT ANSWER: D

Anything that causes firms' costs of production to decrease will increase short-run aggregate supply. Among these choices, a decrease in the prices of commodities would cause a decrease in production costs.

INCORRECT ANSWER

Anything that causes firms' costs of production to decrease will increase short-run aggregate supply. Be careful not to choose a factor that affects aggregate demand.

10. CORRECT ANSWER: C

An increase in nominal wages would increase production costs for producers at any price level. As a result, short-run aggregate supply would decrease, or shift to the left.

INCORRECT ANSWER

Consider how a firm's profits are affected by a increase in wages.

11. CORRECT ANSWER: A

A movement from Point A to Point B represents a rightward shift in short-run aggregate supply, which is caused by an increase in production costs. An increase in the cost of productive resources is the only answer choice that can cause such a shift.

INCORRECT ANSWER

A rightward shift in short-run aggregate supply is caused by an increase in production costs.

12. CORRECT ANSWER: D

An increase in the price of gasoline, a productive input, would cause a decrease in short-run aggregate supply.

INCORRECT ANSWER

Gasoline is an important productive input. What change would be caused by an increase in its price?

13. CORRECT ANSWER: E

When there are new manufacturing standards that producers must meet the cost of production increases to account for product redesigns, new materials needed, and labor-hours needed to adapt the product. These increased costs will cause a leftward shift in short-run aggregate supply.

INCORRECT ANSWER

When a product must meet a new manufacturing standard, it adds to the cost of production.

14. CORRECT ANSWER: C

A movement from Point B to Point E represents a rightward shift in short-run aggregate supply, which is caused by a reduction in production costs. A significant wage reduction would cause such a shift.

INCORRECT ANSWER

A movement from Point B to Point E represents a rightward shift in short-run aggregate supply, which is caused by a reduction in production costs.

15. **CORRECT ANSWER: C**

A movement upward along the SRAS1 curve from Point A to Point B occurs as price level increases.

INCORRECT ANSWER

The movement from Point A to Point B is an upward movement along the SRAS1 curve. Trace this change on the axes of the graph and then inspect the answer choices.

MACROECONOMIC EQUILIBRIUM

TOPIC 1: REAL OUTPUT AND PRICE LEVEL

DIFFICULTY LEVEL 2

1. **CORRECT ANSWER: A**

   An increase in government spending causes a rightward shift in aggregate demand while short-run aggregate supply remains unchanged. Equilibrium price level increases and aggregate output (rGDP) increases.

   INCORRECT ANSWER

   This question is best answered by drawing the AD-AS graph and making the necessary shift. Then trace the changes in equilibrium price level and output to correctly select your answer.

2. **CORRECT ANSWER: A**

   An increase in business optimism and purchases of physical capital represent increases in investment spending, which causes a rightward shift in aggregate demand while short-run aggregate supply remains unchanged. Equilibrium price level increases and aggregate output (rGDP) increases.

   INCORRECT ANSWER

   This question is best answered by drawing the AD-AS graph and making the necessary shift. Then trace the changes in equilibrium price level and output to correctly select your answer.

3. **CORRECT ANSWER: B**

   An increase personal income taxes represents a decrease in consumption spending, which causes a leftward shift in aggregate demand while short-run aggregate supply remains unchanged. Equilibrium price level decreases and aggregate output (rGDP) decreases.

INCORRECT ANSWER

This question is best answered by drawing the AD-AS graph and making the necessary shift. Then trace the changes in equilibrium price level and output to correctly select your answer.

4. **CORRECT ANSWER: B**

The graph demonstrates a leftward shift of the short-run aggregate supply curve. This change is caused by an increase in the cost of production, for which an increase in the price of oil is the only appropriate answer choice.

INCORRECT ANSWER

While there are many changes occuring in the graph, focus on what curve has shifted: short-run aggregate supply has shifted to the left. What answer choice could have caused this?

5. **CORRECT ANSWER: B**

The first shift, in aggregate supply, will cause output to increase and price level to decrease. The second shift, in aggregate demand, will cause output to decrease, possibly beyond where it began before the first shift. The only certainty is that in this second shift the price level will decrease further.

INCORRECT ANSWER

The key to answering this question is to trace the shifts in a methodical manner. Draw the first shift and trace the changes in price level and output, then draw the second shift and trace the changes again. Has price level or output moved in the same direction in both shifts?

6. **CORRECT ANSWER: D**

Stagflation indicates rising unemployment, falling output, and rising prices. This combination of factors is caused by a decrease in short-run aggregate supply—a negative demand shock.

INCORRECT ANSWER

Stagflation indicates rising unemployment, falling output, and rising prices. What type of shift causes these results?

7. CORRECT ANSWER: B

Net exports are a component of aggregate demand. As net exports rise, aggregate demand increases, causing equilibrium output and price level to rise, and the unemployment rate to fall.

Net exports are a component of aggregate demand. As net exports rise, aggregate demand increases. What are the results of such a shift?

DIFFICULTY LEVEL 3

8. CORRECT ANSWER: C

Short-run aggregate supply must shift to the left to achieve the changes in price level and output described by the question. Of the answer choices, an increase in nominal wages would cause such an aggregate supply shift.

INCORRECT ANSWER

First, determine what shift must occur to achieve the changes in price level and output described by the question. Secondly, find the answer choice that causes such a shift. It may help to draw the AD-AS graph and to make notes beside each answer choice to clarify what shift would occur.

9. CORRECT ANSWER: A

The cause of the decrease in aggregate output and price level can only be caused by a decrease in aggregate demand. When AD falls unexpectedly, firms are left with unplanned inventories (i.e. inventories that were produced in anticipation of being demanded).

INCORRECT ANSWER

The first step in answering this question is to determine what shift must occur to achieve the changes in price level and output described by the question. It may be helpful to draw the graph.

10. CORRECT ANSWER: C

Output can only increase if there is an increase in aggregate demand or short-run aggregate supply.

INCORRECT ANSWER

If you are having trouble, test each shift and quickly trace its effect on output to narrow down the answer.

TOPIC 2: SHORT AND LONG RUN

DIFFICULTY LEVEL 2

11. CORRECT ANSWER: B

According to the graph, the economy is experiencing an inflationary gap with a low unemployment rate. In the long-run, nominal wages will rise and the short-run aggregate supply curve will shift to the left to restore long-run equilibrium.

INCORRECT ANSWER

According to the graph, the economy is experiencing an inflationary gap with a low unemployment rate. What is the resulting shift in the long-run?

DIFFICULTY LEVEL 3

12. CORRECT ANSWER: C

In it's current state at Point X, this economy is in recession with high unemployment. In the short-run, wages are fixed, but in the long-run wages will decrease. As wages decrease, short-run aggregate supply will shift to the right to restore long-run equilibrium

INCORRECT ANSWER

At Point X, this economy is in recession. What will begin to happen to wages in the long-run? What shift will occur when wages finally change?

13. CORRECT ANSWER: D

When the stock market increases in value, households feel wealthier and increase their consumption, causing aggregate demand to increase. In the short-run, this will cause an increase in output and a decrease in the unemployment rate. In the long-run, nominal wages will increase causing short-run aggregate supply to decrease and restore long-run equilibrium. In the end, the unemployment level will not have changed.

INCORRECT ANSWER

It is helpful to draw a graph to trace the changes that occur. Begin with an economy in long-run equilibrium and then shift aggregate demand to the right to indicate the increase in the value of the stock market. How has the unemployment rate changed? Now, how will it have changed once the economy adjusts in the long-run?

14. CORRECT ANSWER: B

When the government increases its spending, aggregate supply will increase, causing the price level and output to rise in the short-run. Consequently, nominal wages will increase, causing short-run aggregate supply to shift to the left to restore long-run equilibrium back at the original level out output, but at an even higher price level.

INCORRECT ANSWER

It is helpful to draw a graph to trace the changes that occur. Begin with an economy in long-run equilibrium and then shift aggregate demand to the right to indicate the increase government spending. Now adjust short-run aggregate supply to account for the resulting change in nominal wages and trace the overall effects on output and price level.

TOPIC 3: ACTUAL V. FULL EMPLOYMENT OUTPUT

DIFFICULTY LEVEL 2

15. CORRECT ANSWER: C

When the economy is at long-run equilibrium, the economy is at full employment output and the unemployment rate is equal to the natural rate of unemployment.

INCORRECT ANSWER

In a recession, the economy is producing less than its potential output. Since it is not producing as much as it can, what can be said about the labor market in this economy?

16. CORRECT ANSWER: E

According to the graph, the economy is producing at long-run equilibrium, which means it is producing at its potential output. When producing at potential output, the economy is producing at the natural rate of unemployment. There is no cyclical unemployment, only structural and/or frictional. This is called full employment output.

INCORRECT ANSWER

This economy is producing at long-run equilibrium, or potential output. What can be said about the unemployment rate at this level of production. Remember that even during good times there is still unemployment.

TOPIC 4: BUSINESS CYCLE AND ECONOMIC FLUCTUATIONS

DIFFICULTY LEVEL 2

17. CORRECT ANSWER: B

When short-run equilibrium occurs at a level of output that is less than the potential level of output (where long-run aggregate supply intersects the horizontal axis), the economy is in recession. In a recession, the unemployment rate is high.

INCORRECT ANSWER

The level of output at long-run aggregate supply represents full-employment output, the economy's potential level of output. What is indicated about the level of output at Point X?

18. CORRECT ANSWER: B

A recession occurs when aggregate output is below potential output and the unemployment rate is greater than the natural rate.

INCORRECT ANSWER

When an economy is in recession, how is it producing in relation to its potential level of output? What is the state of the labor market in a recession?

19. CORRECT ANSWER: D

When an economy is in long-run equilibrium, an inflationary gap can be created by an increase in aggregate demand, short-run aggregate supply, or both. An increase in the wealth of households and an increase in government spending would increase AD.

INCORRECT ANSWER

When an economy is in long-run equilibrium, an inflationary gap can be created by an increase in aggregate demand, short-run aggregate supply, or both. Which of these options will create these changes?

Financial Sector

MONEY, BANKING, AND FINANCIAL MARKETS

TOPIC 1: DEFINITION OF FINANCIAL ASSETS: MONEY, STOCKS, BONDS

DIFFICULTY LEVEL 1

20. CORRECT ANSWER: E

A stock represents a share in the ownership of a corporation. These shares are bought and sold in the stock market.

INCORRECT ANSWER

These shares can be bought and sold in a market. Try eliminating a few answers before choosing.

21. CORRECT ANSWER: A

A bond is a type of I.O.U. in which the purchaser is promised future income in addition to a return of the face value of the bond.

INCORRECT ANSWER

Do not confuse bonds, stocks, mortgages, and money—they represent different types of assets.

DIFFICULTY LEVEL 2

22. CORRECT ANSWER: C

Financial assets include money, stocks, bonds, and other non-physical assets. The apartment building and factory, along with productive physical capital like machines and tools, represent physical assets.

INCORRECT ANSWER

Consider that only two of these examples are physical things.

23. CORRECT ANSWER: B

When money is being exchanged for goods or services, it is acting as a medium of exchange.

INCORRECT ANSWER

Try to eliminate some answers that do not quite fit. For example, since Eric is using his money to buy gasoline, he is not storing value since he is giving the money to somebody else.

24. CORRECT ANSWER: D

Money is anything that can be used as a medium of exchange, and its real value is the goods and services for which it can be exchanged. A tempting answer here is the value of the gold backing the money supply, but remember that U.S. currency is fiat money, backed by the its official status as money rather than by any commodity.

INCORRECT ANSWER

In economics, when the term "real value" is used, it refers to purchasing power, i.e. what can actually be purchased.

25. CORRECT ANSWER: E

Gold coins are a commodity that can be used as money or for another purpose, such as making jewelry. When the money supply is changed to notes that represent gold coins held in reserve, those notes are known as commodity-backed money.

INCORRECT ANSWER

A commodity is something that can be consumed or used to produce another good. Considering this definition, then pieces of gold are a commodity.

TOPIC 2: TIME VALUE OF MONEY (PRESENT AND FUTURE VALUE)

DIFFICULTY LEVEL 2

26. CORRECT ANSWER: D

The formula for future value is:

$$Future\ value = Present\ value \times (1 + interest\ rate)^{\#\ of\ years}$$

In this case, the math is simple: $100 X 1.08 = $108.

INCORRECT ANSWER

Try using the formula for future value:

$Future\ value = Present\ value \times (1 + interest\ rate)^{\#\ of\ years}$

DIFFICULTY LEVEL 3

27. CORRECT ANSWER: C

The present value is equal to the future value one year from now ($1.10) divided by one plus the interest rate, which works out to $1.10/1.10, or $1.Another way to think of this is to ask "How much money must I save at 10% interest for one year to equal $1.10?"

INCORRECT ANSWER

Try rephrasing the question as, "How much money must I save at 10% interest for one year to equal $1.10?"

28. CORRECT ANSWER: C

You can use the formula for future value:

$Future\ value = Present\ value \times (1 + interest\ rate)^{\#\ of\ years}$

There is one caveat—you must use the real interest rate of 2%, which is the nominal rate of 5% subtracted by the 3% rate of inflation.

INCORRECT ANSWER

You can use the formula for future value:

$Future\ value = Present\ value \times (1 + interest\ rate)^{\#\ of\ years}$

However, be sure to account for the 2% inflation rate, which will decrease the real future value of the loan.

TOPIC 3: MEASURES OF MONEY SUPPLY

DIFFICULTY LEVEL 1

29. CORRECT ANSWER: E

Gold is not a part of the money supply, although many years ago the United States issued paper currency that was backed by gold reserves.

INCORRECT ANSWER

Use M1 as your measure of what is included and excluded from the money supply.

30. CORRECT ANSWER: A

M1 money includes only the most liquid assets. Currency, traveler's checks, and checkable deposits are the most easily and quickly convertible to a medium of exchange.

INCORRECT ANSWER

Liquidity describes an asset that is easily and quickly convertible into a medium of exchange.

DIFFICULTY LEVEL 2

31. CORRECT ANSWER: D

The M1 money supply consists of currency and coin in circulation, traveler's checks, and checkable deposits. Checkable deposits constitutes the largest of these components.

INCORRECT ANSWER

First eliminate any answer that is not a part of the M1 money supply to narrow your answer.

32. CORRECT ANSWER: A

The withdrawal has no effect on the M1 measure of the money supply because both cash and checkable deposits are part of M1. The $500 withdrawal merely changes the composition of the money.

INCORRECT ANSWER

There are two forms of money in use here: checkable deposits and cash. Are these forms a part of M1, M2, or both?

33. CORRECT ANSWER: E

All the components of M1 are included in M2.. When Nancy withdraws the $2000 from savings and moves it to her checking account, it becomes both M1 and M2. Since it was already counted in M2 initially, there is no change in M2. When the money arrives in the checking account, M1 increases by $2000.

INCORRECT ANSWER

Be sure to trace the movement of money carefully. Remember that all components of M1 are included in M2, but not all components of M2 are included in M1.

34. CORRECT ANSWER: B

M1 includes currency, traveler's checks, and checkable deposits, which totals $100, and M2 includes M1, short time deposits, savings deposits, and money market funds, which totals $160.

INCORRECT ANSWER

It may be helpful to scribble M1 next to each component of that measurement and M2 next to each of its components as well. Remember that all the components of M1 are also in M2.

TOPIC 4: BANKS AND CREATION OF MONEY

DIFFICULTY LEVEL 1

35. CORRECT ANSWER: D

When a bank deposit is made, banks often loan or invest much of the deposit. The fraction of the deposit that is held as a liquid asset like currency or held in deposit at the Federal Reserve are called bank reserves.

INCORRECT ANSWER

It is important to understand that banks do not hold all of the cash a customer deposits in a vault.

36. CORRECT ANSWER: C

The reserve ratio measures the ratio of reserves to deposits. For instance, if $100 has been deposited and the bank holds $20 in reserve, then the reserve ratio is 0.2.

INCORRECT ANSWER

Consider that a bank reserves are deposits kept as currency or on deposit at the Federal Reserve.

DIFFICULTY LEVEL 2

37. CORRECT ANSWER: C

The bank must hold 10% of $200, or $20, in reserve. It can loan out the remaining $180 if it chooses to.

INCORRECT ANSWER

The required reserve ratio indicates what percentage of deposits must be held as reserves. What remains can be loaned.

38. CORRECT ANSWER: D

Since the required reserve ratio is 10 percent, the money multiplier equals 1/0.1, or By multiplying the $25 deposit by this money multiplier, we can determine that the maximum possible change in demand deposits in the banking system is $250.

INCORRECT ANSWER

The first step in determining the answer is to calculate the money multiplier. The formula fo rthe money multiplier is $\frac{1}{required\ reserve\ ratio}$.

39. CORRECT ANSWER: A

To create money a bank must issue a loan. When a deposit is made at the bank, currency is converted into a demand deposit. In order to increase the money supply, some of that deposit is converted into a liquid asset such as currency and loaned to a customer.

INCORRECT ANSWER

When a deposit is made, currency is taken out of circulation and converted into a demand deposit. How can a bank use that currency be used to add to the money supply.

40. CORRECT ANSWER: D

The maximum expansion of the money supply through the multiple deposit expansion process can be determined using the money multiplier: $\frac{1}{required\ reserve\ ratio}$. In this case, the money multiplier is 5, which is multiplied by the $50 of excess reserves to get $250.

INCORRECT ANSWER

The maximum expansion of the money supply through the multiple deposit expansion process can be determined using the money multiplier: $\frac{1}{required\ reserve\ ratio}$.

41. CORRECT ANSWER: D

The more money that is deposited at a bank, the greater the amount of money that can be loaned by the bank. If the public increases its money holdings, less money will be deposited in banks, reducing the ability of banks to expand credit.

INCORRECT ANSWER

If the public is holding more money as currency, then less money is being deposited into banks. How does this change the abilities of the banking system?

42. CORRECT ANSWER: D

Since the bank has no excess reserves to begin with, a $200 deposit will create $160 of excess reserves because 20% of the $200 deposit, or $40, fulfills the reserve requirement.

INCORRECT ANSWER

This bank is required to reserve 20% of all deposits. How much must be reserved of the $200 deposit? How much remains after the required reserves are accounted for?

43. CORRECT ANSWER: B

Since the bank has no excess reserves to begin with, a $10,000 deposit will create $8,000 of excess reserves because 20% of the deposit, or $2,000, fulfills the reserve requirement. The bank can loan all of its excess reserves.

INCORRECT ANSWER

This bank is required to reserve 20% of all deposits and it can loan what remains.

44. CORRECT ANSWER: B

According to the data, the bank is holding $15,000 as required reserves out of $100,000 on deposit, making the reserve requirement 15%.

INCORRECT ANSWER

The bank must hold a portion of deposits as required reserves. What percentage of deposits are being held as required reserves in this bank?

DIFFICULTY LEVEL 3

45. CORRECT ANSWER: C

If the bank's excess reserves increased by $850, what became of the remaining $150? The $150, 15% of the $1000 deposit, are the required reserves.

INCORRECT ANSWER

If the bank's excess reserves increased by $850, what became of the remaining $150?

46. CORRECT ANSWER: C

The bank has already invested $75,000 in securities and loaned $12,000. The question states that no securities will be sold, so that $75,000 cannot be converted to money and loaned. The bank only has $13,000 left and it must reserve 11%, or $11,000, which leaves only $2,000 to possibly loan.

INCORRECT ANSWER

Focus on the relevant information: the bank has $100,000 on deposit and must reserve 11% of it. How much of the $100,000 remains as loanable funds?

47. CORRECT ANSWER: C

Use the formula to find the money multiplier: $\frac{1}{required\ reserve\ ratio}$. By multiplying $5,000 by the money multiplier (10), we can find that the maximum multiple deposit expansion of the money supply is $50,000. However, that $50,000 expansion is only achieved if customers do not hold any money and banks do not hold excess reserves. Since the question states that banks will keep some excess reserves, the increase in the money supply will be less than the $50,000 maximum.

INCORRECT ANSWER

Multiply $5,000 by the money multiplier to determine the maximum multiple deposit expansion of the money supply. If banks decide to hold excess reserves, will the money supply expand by the maximum amount?

TOPIC 5: MONEY DEMAND

DIFFICULTY LEVEL 1

48. CORRECT ANSWER: A

When money is held as a very liquid asset, such as cash or a checkable deposit, the opportunity cost is having the money deposited in an interest-bearing savings account, money market account, or invested in bonds.

INCORRECT ANSWER

If one is not holding money as currency, where can the money be deposited? What is the advantage of keeping money on deposit at a bank?

DIFFICULTY LEVEL 2

49. CORRECT ANSWER: D

When national income increases, consumption spending increases and more money is demanded to make transactions.

INCORRECT ANSWER

As incomes increase, people need more money for transactions.

50. CORRECT ANSWER: A

With a higher price level, the public must hold more money to pay for goods and services.

INCORRECT ANSWER

Would you change the amount of cash you keep in your wallet if prices were higher?

51. CORRECT ANSWER: D

An increase in the use of technology that makes transactions more efficient reduces the demand for money. If people increasingly used phones to transfer money to sellers then more money could be left in interest-bearing accounts. Individuals would hold less cash.

INCORRECT ANSWER

If you could pay for everything with your phone, would you carry as much cash?

52. CORRECT ANSWER: E

While the answer may seem counter-intuitive, money demand will increase as ATMs grow more expensive to use. If bank customers find it more expensive to withdraw money at ATMs, they must go to the bank to access their money. Since a trip to the bank is less convenient, customers will withdraw and hold more cash to reduce the necessary number of trips to the bank.

In general, the more access people have to banking and payment technology, the lower their money demand.

INCORRECT ANSWER

If you stopped using ATMs, how much cash would you keep in your wallet?

53. CORRECT ANSWER: C

As the nominal interest rate increases, the opportunity cost of holding money increases. Households and firms will increase the quantity of money deposited in interest-bearing accounts at as interest rates increase.

INCORRECT ANSWER

If you could earn more interest by keeping money deposited in a bank, would you deposit more money or hold more money as cash in your wallet?

TOPIC 6: MONEY MARKET AND THE EQUILIBRIUM NOMINAL INTEREST RATE

54. CORRECT ANSWER: D

According to the money market, as money demand increases (due to the public increasing its money holdings), the equilibrium interest rate rises.

INCORRECT ANSWER

It may be helpful to draw the money market model and shift money demand to the right. What factor changes as a result?

55. CORRECT ANSWER: C

The quantity of money demanded exceeds the quantity of money supplied when the interest rate is below equilibrium. At this low interest rate, investors will want to withdraw money from interest-bearing assets and increase their money holdings, which will drive up interest rates.

INCORRECT ANSWER

Try to think of money as a type of good. If there is a higher quantity demanded of a good than there is supplied, what changes?

56. CORRECT ANSWER: A

If there is an increase in the money supply, the line that represents it on the graph will shift to the right. Since money demand does not change, the new equilibrium nominal interest rate will decrease.

INCORRECT ANSWER

Use the provided graph to help determine the answer. What is the result when the money supply curve shifts to the right?

57. CORRECT ANSWER: D

To cause a decrease in the money market, money demand must decrease and/or the money supply must increase. An expansionary monetary policy causes an increase in the money supply and a decrease in price level causes a decrease in money demand.

If there was an increase in real gross domestic product, then consumption would increase, causing money demand to increase, thus eliminating this change as a correct option.

INCORRECT ANSWER

Test each of the three changes on the graph to see which would cause the nominal interest rate to decrease. This type of question often appears on the AP exam without the aid of a graph, so you may need to draw your own.

LOANABLE FUNDS MARKET

TOPIC 1: SUPPLY OF AND DEMAND FOR LOANABLE FUNDS

DIFFICULTY LEVEL 1

1. CORRECT ANSWER: B

The cost of a investment project includes the prices of any goods and services purchased plus the cost of the loaned funds. As the cost of borrowing funds decreases, the rate of return of an investment project increases.

INCORRECT ANSWER

Firms are more likely to conduct investment spending if they are more assured of making a profit. What factor increases the liklihood of making a profit on an investment project?

2. CORRECT ANSWER: D

Savers and borrowers interact in the loanable funds market. Savers are, in essence, the lenders in the market and firms, consumers, and the government comprise the borrowers. The financial system connects savers and borrowers by providing loans at market interest rates.

INCORRECT ANSWER

Since the model refers to loanable funds, the agents involved must be loaning or borrowing funds. Which of the answer choices best describes lenders and borrowers?

DIFFICULTY LEVEL 2

3. CORRECT ANSWER: E

A movement from Point A to Point C represents an increase in the demand for loanable funds, which occurs when there is an increased desire to borrow. When firms become more optimistic about future business opportunities, they increase their borrowing to pay for new investment spending.

INCORRECT ANSWER

A movement from Point A to Point C represents an increase in the demand for loanable funds, which occurs when there is an increased desire to borrow.

4. **CORRECT ANSWER: B**

A movement from Point E to Point B represents a decrease in the demand for loanable funds, which occurs when there is a decreased desire to borrow. When the government decreases its spending and runs a budget surplus, a major demand for loanable funds decreases.

INCORRECT ANSWER

A movement from Point E to Point B represents a decrease in the demand for loanable funds, which occurs when there is a decreased desire to borrow.

5. **CORRECT ANSWER: D**

Savings represent the supply of loanable funds. Domestic savings decrease as people move their assets to foreign financial institutions, so the supply of loanable funds decreases in the domestic loanable funds market.

INCORRECT ANSWER

Remember that savings represent the supply of loanable funds.

DIFFICULTY LEVEL 3

6. **CORRECT ANSWER: C**

If financial institutions offer an interest rate that is higher than the current interest rate, the quantity of loanable funds supplied will increase since there is a greater incentive to deposit savings to earn more interest.

INCORRECT ANSWER

If you were offered a higher price for something that you own, would you be more likely to offer it for sale? What happens when banks offer a higher price for your savings— would you supply the bank with more of your savings?

TOPIC 2: EQUILIBRIUM REAL INTEREST RATE

DIFFICULTY LEVEL 2

7. CORRECT ANSWER: E

If there is a decrease in perceived business opportunities then the demand for loanable funds will decrease, causing the equilibrium real interest rate to decrease.

INCORRECT ANSWER

If firms believe there will be fewer business opportunities in the future, they will decrease their borrowing. It may be helpful to graph the shifting demand curve for loanable funds to better trace the effect on the equilibrium real interest rate.

8. CORRECT ANSWER: C

In the loanable funds market, savers are suppliers of loanable funds. An increase in savings will increase the supply of loanable funds and decrease the real interest rate.

INCORRECT ANSWER

Are savers suppliers or demanders of loanable funds?

9. CORRECT ANSWER: B

An increase in construction projects would increase the demand for loanable funds as housing developers must increase their borrowing to fund the projects. This increased demand wil drive up the real interest rate. The remaining choices involve either a decrease in demand or an increase in supply of loanable funds.

INCORRECT ANSWER

As in any market, an increase in demand or a decrease in supply will drive down price. In the loanable funds market, the price is represented by the real interest rate.

DIFFICULTY LEVEL 1

10. CORRECT ANSWER: D

Crowding out occurs when the government competes with the private sector in demanding loanable funds, resulting in an increase in the real interest rate and a decrease in private investment.

INCORRECT ANSWER

Think of crowding out as too much demand for a limited supply. Who competes with the public in demanding loanable funds?

11. CORRECT ANSWER: B

Crowding out occurs when government borrowing increases demand for loanable funds, driving up interest rates and causing a decrease in private sector investment.

INCORRECT ANSWER

If the government increases borrowing, it is increasing the demand for loanable funds. What is the effect on interest rates? What is the result for private investors who are also seeking to borrow loanable funds?

DIFFICULTY LEVEL 2

12. CORRECT ANSWER: D

If the national government is conducting deficit spending, it must be funding that spending with increased borrowing. The increase in demand for loanable funds will increase the real interest rate, which makes investment more expensive for everyone else.

INCORRECT ANSWER

If the national government is conducting deficit spending, it must be funding that spending with increased borrowing. What is the result of this increased borrowing on the real interest rate? Will others be as likely to borrow and invest?

CORRECT ANSWER: D

Crowding out is defined as a decrease in investment spending that results from an increase in government borrowing and interest rates. An increase in the budget deficit is a direct cause of increased government borrowing.

INCORRECT ANSWER

Crowding out refers to an increase in interest rates due to increased competition for loanable funds. Which of these choices represents an increase in demand for loanable funds?

14. **CORRECT ANSWER: D**

Expansionary fiscal policies move the government budget balance toward deficit, requiring the government to increase its demand for loanable funds. This shift in the loanable funds market causes interest rates to rise.

INCORRECT ANSWER

When the government implements an expansionary fiscal policy, it spends more and taxes less, which results in an increase in the budget deficit. How does the government's increase in borrowing affect the loanable funds market?

CENTRAL BANK AND CONTROL OF THE MONEY SUPPLY

TOPIC 1: TOOLS OF CENTRAL BANK POLICY

DIFFICULTY LEVEL 1

1. CORRECT ANSWER: C

Despite its influence on the money supply, the Federal Reserve System does not conduct monetary policy by minting bills and coins.

INCORRECT ANSWER

Monetary policy refers to the government's control of the money supply. However, try not to take "control of the money supply" too literally. The Federal Reserve System conducts monetary policy mainly by influencing the financial system.

2. CORRECT ANSWER: C

The Federal Reserve is known as the "lender of last resort" because it can loan funds to banks that have fallen short on reserves. When a bank borrows from the Fed, it does so at the discount rate.

INCORRECT ANSWER

Some of the answer choices can be eliminated based on basic knowledge of the functions of the Federal Reserve System. For instance, the Fed does not sell goods and services.

DIFFICULTY LEVEL 2

3. CORRECT ANSWER: E

When the Fed conducts a sale of treasury bills, banks purchase the bills with their excess reserves, exchanging their money assets for the non-money treasury bills. With lower levels of reserves, banks will charge higher interest rates to other banks and to customers.

4. **CORRECT ANSWER: B**

To increase the money supply with open market operations, the Fed must purchase U.S. Treasury bills, or bonds. The increase in demand for bonds will drive up the price of bonds.

INCORRECT ANSWER

Open market operations involve the purchase or sale of U.S. Treasury bills, or bonds.

5. **CORRECT ANSWER: E**

A decrease in both the reserve requirement and the discount rate would cause the greatest increase in the money supply. With a lower reserve requirement, banks will be permitted to loan a greater percentage of their reserves. With a lower discount rate, banks can reduce the cost of borrowing reserves, encouraging them to increase their lending.

INCORRECT ANSWER

To increase the money supply, the Fed enables banks to increase their lending. What changes in the reserve requirement and the discount rate would encourage banks to loan more money?

6. **CORRECT ANSWER: C**

A decrease in the discount rate enables banks to borrow excess reserves at a lower price, encouraging them to increase lending. The increase in lending will increase the money supply and put downward pressure on interest rates.

INCORRECT ANSWER

The discount rate affects banks' costs of borrowing reserves. How does the money market change when banks have the ability to borrow reserves at a lower cost?

7. **CORRECT ANSWER: D**

Banks can create money by issuing loans. By decreasing the reserve requirement, banks will be permitted to loan a greater percentage of their reserves.

INCORRECT ANSWER

Remember that banks create money by issuing loans. Which of the answer choices will enable banks do increase their lending?

8. **CORRECT ANSWER: C**

When the Fed conducts a sale of bonds in the open market, the money supply will decrease and cause interest rates to increase.

Choices A and D can immediately be eliminated as answer choices because they indicate fiscal policies rather than monetary policies.

INCORRECT ANSWER

Be sure to distinguish between monetary and fiscal policies. Then narrow the your choices further by selecting only policies that will decrease the money supply.

TOPIC 2: QUANTITY THEORY OF MONEY

DIFFICULTY LEVEL 1

9. **CORRECT ANSWER: B**

Use the monetary equation of exchange, based on the quantity theory of money: $MV = PY$, in which M is the money supply, V is the velocity of money, P is the price level, and Y is real GDP. Remember that the product of price level and real GDP is nominal GDP, so \$1,200 comprises the entire right side of the equation.

INCORRECT ANSWER

Same as above.

10. **CORRECT ANSWER: C**

Use the monetary equation of exchange, based on the quantity theory of money: $MV = PY$, in which M is the money supply, V is the velocity of money, P is the price level, and Y is real GDP.

It is important to remember that according to the quantity theory of money, the velocity of money is constant, as is real output. So, an increase in the money supply must cause an increase only in price level.

INCORRECT ANSWER

Remember the monetary equation of exchange, based on the quantity theory of money: $MV = PY$, in which M is the money supply, V is the velocity of money, P is the price level, and Y is real GDP. Also, according to the theory, the velocity of money and real GDP are both constant.

DIFFICULTY LEVEL 2

11. CORRECT ANSWER: E

Use the monetary equation of exchange: $MV = PY$. If V is constant, then a decrease in the money supply (M) must lead to a decrease in PY. Price level multiplied by real output is equal to nominal output, so nominal output must be decreasing.

INCORRECT ANSWER

Use the monetary equation of exchange: $MV = PY$, but remember that PY is equal to nominal real domestic product.

TOPIC 3: REAL V. NOMINAL INTEREST RATES

DIFFICULTY LEVEL 1

12. CORRECT ANSWER: D

The nominal interest rate is equal to the real interest rate plus the expected inflation rate. In this case, the lender should charge 8 percent interest to receive 5 percent of real interest after the expected 3 percent inflation rate reduces the nominal value of the loan.

INCORRECT ANSWER

Remember that the real interest rate is what the lender hopes to make after accounting for inflation.

13. CORRECT ANSWER: D

The change in real wages is equal to the change in nominal wages minus the inflation rate. In this case, the worker receives a 25 percent nominal increase in wage rate but 10 percent inflation reduces the real wage rate change to an increase of only 15 percent.

INCORRECT ANSWER

A raise from $8 to $10 per hour is a 25 percent raise. If inflation is 10 percent, what does that raise really feel like to the worker when making purchases?

14. CORRECT ANSWER: A

The expected inflation rate is the nominal interest rate minus the real interest rate. Another way to consider this problem is to reason that the bank really hopes to earn 5 percent on the loan, so it will charge the borrower an additional 3 percent to account for inflation, making the nominal price of the loan 8 percent.

INCORRECT ANSWER

If you can't remember the formula, try to think of the problem in different words. The bank really wants to earn 5 percent interest, but the price they name for the loan is 8 percent—why?

15. CORRECT ANSWER: C

Anna expects to be repaid with an amount that is equal to the real value of the $100 today. The nominal value she must be repaid is equal to the real value plus the expected rate of inflation. $100 plus 8 percent equals $108.

INCORRECT ANSWER

Assume that Anna wants to buy a stereo that costs $100. How much will that stereo cost in one year if prices increase by 8 percent? If she lends the $100 for one year, how much should she demand in repayment?

Stabilization Policies

FISCAL AND MONETARY POLICIES

TOPIC 1: DEMAND-SIDE EFFECTS

DIFFICULTY LEVEL 1

1. **CORRECT ANSWER: B**

   The government engages in fiscal policy when it makes changes in spending or changes in taxation. In the United States, these changes are typically conducted by Congress and the President, though state and local governments may engage in these policies as well.

   Be sure to distinguish fiscal policy from the monetary policy conducted by the Federal Reserve System.

2. **CORRECT ANSWER: C**

   Changes in personal income taxes are a tool of fiscal policy, while the remaining choices are monetary policies conducted by the Federal Reserve System.

   INCORRECT ANSWER

   Monetary policy includes changes by the Federal Reserve System that affect the banking system's abiity to create money. Which of the choices does not fulfill these criterial.

DIFFICULTY LEVEL 2

3. **CORRECT ANSWER: D**

   To combat inflation, a contractionary policy is needed to decrease aggregate demand. Be careful not to select a monetary policy, as the question specifies to choose a fiscal policy. An increase in taxes is the only answer to fulfill the criteria.

   INCORRECT ANSWER

   Be sure to select a contractionary fiscal policy.

4. **CORRECT ANSWER: D**

If cyclical unemployment exists, then the economy is in recession. An expansionary policy is needed to decrease unemployment. An increase in government spending is the only choice that would achieve the necessary increase in output.

INCORRECT ANSWER

If cyclical unemployment exists then the economy is in recession.

5. **CORRECT ANSWER: D**

According to the graph, this economy is experiencing a recession. The appropriate fiscal policy is to increase aggregate demand by decreasing personal income taxes.

INCORRECT ANSWER

According to the graph, the economy's current output (Y) is less than its potential output (Yp). This signifies that the economy is in recession. What fiscal policy can correct this?

6. **CORRECT ANSWER: B**

An increase in government spending will increase aggregate demand, causing it to shift to the right. This shift will have the effect of increasing the aggregate price level and output.

INCORRECT ANSWER

Start by shifting aggregate demand on the graph then trace the resulting changes in equilibrium price level and output.

7. **CORRECT ANSWER: B**

A decrease of the reserve requirement by the Fed would lead to an increase in the money supply and a decrease in interest rates. This decrease in interest rates would result in an increase in investment spending, such as businesses increasing purchases of capital goods.

INCORRECT ANSWER

When the Fed lowers the reserve requirement, banks are able to increase their lending. An increase in loans will increase the money supply. What changes result when there is an increase in the money supply?

8. **CORRECT ANSWER: C**

The combined effects of these two fiscal changes is an increase in aggregate demand. The decrease in taxes and increase in government spending will cause an increase in purchases of goods and services. As consumption increases, output will increase and unemployment will decrease.

INCORRECT ANSWER

If taxes decrease, households and firms will have more disposable income. Combined with an increase in government spending, how will consumption and unemployment be affected?

9. **CORRECT ANSWER: D**

Both a decrease in aggregate demand and a decrease in short-run aggregate supply result in a decrease in output. To correctly determine the answer, simply test each of the four changes by drawing the changes on the accompanying graph and tracing the changes in output.

INCORRECT ANSWER

To correctly determine the answer, simply test each of the four changes by drawing the changes on the accompanying graph and tracing the changes in output.

10. **CORRECT ANSWER: E**

To reduce an inflationary gap, aggregate demand or short-run aggregate supply must decrease. All of the choices affect aggregate demand, and among them only an increase in the income tax rate would decrease aggregate supply.

INCORRECT ANSWER

To reduce an inflationary gap, the price level must decrease. The only changes that can cause a price level decrease are a decrease in aggregate demand or a decrease in short-run aggregate supply. Most government policies only have an effect on aggregate demand.

11. **CORRECT ANSWER: A**

A decrease in the money supply will cause the real interest rate to decrease, resulting in a decrease in investment spending (and interest-sensitive consumption spending). This decrease in spending will decrease aggregate demand and real output.

INCORRECT ANSWER

When the money supply decreases, it has an effect on interest rates that then causes changes in interest-sensitive spending, such as purchases of real estate, physical capital, or automobiles.

Start this question by considering how a decrease in the money supply affects interest rates and go from there!

12. CORRECT ANSWER: E

A recessionary gap can be eliminated by an expansionary policy, which increases aggregate demand and results in an increase in output.

The only answer that would not result in these changes is a decrease in the money supply. Such a change would cause interest rates to rise, investment spending to decrease, a decrease in aggregate demand, and a decrease in output that would worsen the recession.

INCORRECT ANSWER

A recessionary gap can be eliminated by an expansionary policy, which increases aggregate demand and results in an increase in output. All of these answer choices fit these criteria but one.

13. CORRECT ANSWER: A

The question describes an increase in exports and a decrease in imports, which is to say there is an increase in net exports (net exports = exports – imports). If net exports are increasing, then aggregate demand is increasing, which results in an increase in output and price level, and a decrease in the unemployment rate.

INCORRECT ANSWER

The question describes an increase in exports and a decrease in imports, which is to say there is an increase in net exports (net exports = exports – imports). How does this affect aggregate demand, output, price level, and unemployment?

14. CORRECT ANSWER: C

A contractionary fiscal policy causes aggregate demand to decrease, or shift to the left. By drawing an AD-AS graph and tracing the changes, it can be concluded that price level and output will decrease.

A contractionary fiscal policy causes aggregate demand to decrease, or shift to the left. Draw an AD-AS graph and trace the changes in price level and output to narrow down the correct answer.

15. CORRECT ANSWER: D

A negative shock would most likely cause a recession. Of the changes listed, only an open market sale by the Federal Reserve would cause a negative shock. This bond sale is a contractionary monetary policy that would decrease aggregate demand and lead toward recession.

A negative shock would cause the economy to fall into recession. Which answer choice describes a decrease in aggregate supply or demand?

16. CORRECT ANSWER: C

An increase in purchases of capital stock represents an increase in investment spending, which causes aggregate demand to increase. The only factor that decreases with an increase in AD is the unemployment rate, as more workers will be hired to produce additional output.

An increase in purchases of capital stock represents an increase in investment spending, which causes aggregate demand to increase. Which factor decreases when AD increases?

17. CORRECT ANSWER: A

If the Federal Reserve uses monetary policy to reduce inflation, it must decrease the money supply, resulting in an increase in interest rates, a decrease in aggregate demand, and a decrease in price level.

To reduce inflation, the Federal Reserve must use monetary policy to reduce aggregate demand.

18. CORRECT ANSWER: A

A decrease in the real interest rate reduces the cost of borrowing funds, which causes an increase in interest-sensitive spending, such as auto purchases. If consumption spending increases, aggregate demand shifts to the right and real GDP increases as well.

INCORRECT ANSWER

A change in the real interest rate affects interest-sensitive spending, such as purchases of physical capital and pricey consumer goods like automobiles. How will a decrease in this rate affect consumption and output?

19. CORRECT ANSWER: B

To address a recession, the Fed will likely use an expansionary monetary policy to increase the money supply, lower interest rates, and increase aggregate demand, which would result in an increase in output. Monetary policy is discretionary. The Federal Reserve Board is not required by law to respond to a recession.

INCORRECT ANSWER

The Fed will likely use an expansionary monetary policy to address a recession. How can it increase the money supply?

DIFFICULTY LEVEL 3

20. CORRECT ANSWER: D

Equal increases in taxes and government spending will have the net effect of increasing aggregate demand, which will increase aggregate output in the short-run. While increasing taxes will decrease aggregate demand, it will do so by a smaller factor than the equal increase in government spending.

This difference in the effects of government spending and taxes is because the government will directly spend X dollars, which will multiply by a factor of 1/(1-MPC), but the tax increase will only reduce spending by a factor of (-MPC/MPS). In other words, government spending has a greater multiplier effect than does a change in taxation. The net effect of the changes in answer choice D is a slight increase in aggregate demand.

INCORRECT ANSWER

Each answer choice seems to decrease aggregate output. The correct answer has the net effect of increasing it slightly.

21. CORRECT ANSWER: E

To combat unemployment with an increase in investment spending, policymakers must enact a particular type of expansionary policy—one that causes a decrease in interest rates. In order to have a decrease in interest rates, one component of the policy must include an increase in the money supply. The only answer choice that meets these criteria is an increase in purchases of U.S. Treasury bonds by the Federal Reserve.

INCORRECT ANSWER

To cause an increase in investment spending, a particular type of expansionary policy is necessary—one that causes a decrease in interest rates.

22. CORRECT ANSWER: B

An increase in government spending of $50 billion will increase output by a factor of $50 billion X the spending multiplier. To preserve the unemployment rate, a contractionary policy must be used to counteract this expansionary policy. An increase in taxes can counteract the government spending, but only if the tax increase is by more than $50 billion, as the tax multiplier is always smaller than the spending multiplier.

Remember, the tax multiplier is smaller than the spending multiplier because not all of the taxed funds would have been used for consumption. All of the government's $50 billion was used for consumption.

INCORRECT ANSWER

If the government wants to increase spending without affecting the unemployment rate, it must counteract its expansionary policy with a contractionary one, such as an increase in taxes. However, remember that an increase in spending of $50 billion will actually create a larger increase in output than $50 billion due to the spending multiplier effect.

Does a change in taxes multiply in the economy the same way that a change in government spending does?

TOPIC 2: SUPPLY-SIDE EFFECTS

DIFFICULTY LEVEL 1

23. CORRECT ANSWER: D

In the market for clothing, if the cost of a productive input increases, then the cost of production increases and profits decrease at all prices. These changes result in a decrease in supply, which causes an increase in the equilibrium price of clothing and a decrease in the quantity sold.

Keep in mind that this question regards a microeconomic model of the clothing market, not the macroeconomic aggregate demand-aggregate supply model. Nonetheless, this question is illustrative of the effect of a rising input cost on profits and production.

INCORRECT ANSWER

In the market for clothing, if the cost of a productive input increases, then the cost of production increases and profits decrease at all prices. What will result from these changes in the microeconomic model of the clothing market?

DIFFICULTY LEVEL 2

24. CORRECT ANSWER: B

A decrease in the prices of inputs causes an increase in aggregate supply, so eliminate any answer choices that cause a change in aggregate demand, and eliminate any answer choices that cause anything other than an increase in aggregate supply. Now you have a 50% chance of answering correctly! Draw an AD-AS graph and shift AS to the right to trace the effect on price level.

INCORRECT ANSWER

A decrease in the prices of inputs causes an increase in aggregate supply, so eliminate any answer choices that cause a change in aggregate demand, and eliminate any answer choices that cause anything other than an increase in aggregate supply. Now you have a 50% chance of answering correctly! Draw an AD-AS graph and shift AS to the right to trace the effect on price level.

25. CORRECT ANSWER: D

Stagflation has two symptoms, as suggested by its name. "Stag" refers to a stagnating economy, i.e. declining output. The second part, "-flation", refers to inflation. Declining output and a rising price level is caused by a decrease in aggregate supply.

INCORRECT ANSWER

Stagflation has two symptoms, as suggested by its name. "Stag" refers to a stagnating economy, i.e. declining output. The second part, "-flation", refers to inflation. What shift causes these results?

26. **CORRECT ANSWER: C**

An economy is in recession when it is currently producing a level of real output that is less than its potential output. When producing at potential output, an economy's unemployment is equal to its natural rate. Different economies have a different natural rate of unemployment.

INCORRECT ANSWER

It is easy to surmise that a recession includes some unemployment and a lack of output. How much unemployment? How does real GDP relate to potential output in a recession?

27. **CORRECT ANSWER: B**

It is helpful draw the model described by the question and trace the current level of output to see how it relates to the level of output at long-run aggregate supply, which represents potential output, the natural rate of unemployment, and full-employment output.

Since current output is greater than potential, it can be concluded that there is an inflationary gap, the unemployment rate is less than the natural rate, and the economy is producing beyond full-employment output.

INCORRECT ANSWER

It is helpful draw the model described by the question and trace the current level of output to see how it relates to the level of output at long-run aggregate supply, which represents potential output, the natural rate of unemployment, and full-employment output.

28. **CORRECT ANSWER: D**

An increase in labor productivity would decrease production costs and increase aggregate supply. As a result, output would increase and price level would decrease.

INCORRECT ANSWER

An increase in labor productivity would decrease production costs and increase aggregate supply. Draw an AD-AS graph to trace the effects of such a shift and narrow down your answer.

29. CORRECT ANSWER: D

A contractionary supply shock, or a decrease in aggregate supply, causes a decrease in output, which results in an increase in unemployment.

INCORRECT ANSWER

A contractionary supply shock is a leftward shift of the aggregage supply curve. Try drawing this shift to trace the changes in price level and output, which will help you narrow down your answer choices.

30. CORRECT ANSWER: D

A decrease in the world supply of oil would cause an increase in the equilibrium price of oil. Since oil is a productive input in widespread use, an increase in its price will cause aggregate supply to decrease. A decrease in AS will cause a decrease in output and an increase in price level.

INCORRECT ANSWER

If the world supply of oil decreases, then the price of oil will increase. How will an increase in price for this vital productive resource affect the macroeconomy?

31. CORRECT ANSWER: D

If firms can produce more efficiently at a lower cost, aggregate supply will increase, causing a decrease in the price level and an increase in real output.

INCORRECT ANSWER

Remember, any change that results in producers reducing their production costs will increase aggregate supply.

32. CORRECT ANSWER: B

A positive supply shock decreases production costs throughout the economy, which increases profits and encourages an increase in output at all price levels. As short-run aggregate supply increases, output increases and price level decreases.

INCORRECT ANSWER

A positive supply shock translates to an increase in short-run aggregate supply. Draw an AD-AS graph and trace the changes in output and price level.

33. CORRECT ANSWER: D

A decrease in inflation and unemployment requires an increase in short-run aggregate supply. Among the answer choices, only an increase in labor productivity will achieve this result, as it will decrease production costs and encourage firms to produce more output at any price level.

INCORRECT ANSWER

Draw an AD-AS graph and try shifting AD and SRAS to determine what single shift can cause price level to decrease and output to increase (which causes a lower unemployment rate). Once you know what shift you're seeking, choose the answer choice that causes that shift.

34. CORRECT ANSWER: C

The specific rate changes included in the question are unecessary to select the correct answer. All one needs to know is that unemployment increased while inflation increased. In other words, this economy has experienced stagflation, which is caused by a decrease, or leftward shift, of short-run aggregate supply.

INCORRECT ANSWER

The specific rate changes included in the question are unecessary to select the correct answer. All one needs to know is that unemployment increased while inflation increased. What type of shift causes these results?

35. CORRECT ANSWER: D

A combination of high inflation and high unemployment results from a decrease in short-run aggregate supply, i.e. a negative supply shock. An increase in factor prices, such as for a natural resource like oil, would cause such a supply shock.

INCORRECT ANSWER

Only one type of shift can lead to a simultaneous increase in price level and unemployment—a negative supply shock. Which answer describes a cause of such a shift?

36. CORRECT ANSWER: B

This question is best answered by drawing an AD-AS graph and tracing the two shifts and their effects. The first shift, a decrease in AD, will decrease output and price level. The second shift, an increase in AS, will increase output and further decrease the price level.

The only certainty is that price level will have decreased overall. Since output decreases and then increases, it is not certain what the net effect on output is without quantatative information.

INCORRECT ANSWER

This question is best answered by drawing an AD-AS graph and tracing the two shifts and their effects. Be sure to choose an answer whose results *will definitely* occur, not an answer whose results *could* occur.

37. CORRECT ANSWER: C

Were nominal wages to increase immediately when inflation occurs, then the short-run aggregate supply curve would be vertical. If the price of labor were to rise immediately with inflation, there would be no incentive for producers to increase or decrease output, as their cost of production would remain unchanged.

INCORRECT ANSWER

If prices are rising, producers increase their output because they can earn more profit—assuming their costs remain fixed. Under what conditions will they not earn an increase in profits when prices rise?

38. CORRECT ANSWER: D

The economy is starting in recession. If no policy action is taken, then lingering unemployment will eventually cause nominal wages to decrease and short-run aggregate supply will shift to the right. When this shift occurs, price level will decrease and output will increase.

INCORRECT ANSWER

To correctly choose the changes in price level and output you must first understand the starting place of this economy: in recession. What adjustment occurs in the long-run when an economy is in recession?

39. CORRECT ANSWER: B

The initial shift of aggregate demand to the right will increase price level and real GDP. When the economy adjusts in the long-run, short-run aggregate supply will decrease causing price level to increase further and real GDP to decrease back to the original level of output.

INCORRECT ANSWER

Assume this economy begins in long-run equilibrium. What follows are two shifts: the initial shift of aggregate demand, and then a second shift of aggregate supply that adjusts the economy in the long-run.

40. CORRECT ANSWER: B

The economy depicted in the graph is in recession. In the long-run, when wages become flexible, they will decrease. With lower wages, producers will earn more profit at any price level, causing aggregate supply to shift to the right, creating a new equilibrium equal to full employment.

INCORRECT ANSWER

The economy depicted in the graph is in recession, which indicates that the unemployment rate is greater than it would be at full employment. In the long-run, when wages become flexible, they will decrease.

How will a decrease in nominal wages affect the economy?

41. CORRECT ANSWER: B

This economy is experiencing an inflationary gap. In the long-run, wages will become flexible and increase, causing short-run aggregate supply to shift to the left, moving the economy to long-run equilibrium.

INCORRECT ANSWER

In the long-run, short-run aggregate supply will shift to restore long-run equilibrium. What change in the economy will cause SRAS to shift?

DIFFICULTY LEVEL 3

42. CORRECT ANSWER: C

A negative supply shock will cause an increase in the price level. Although workers may desire a wage increase, it is unlikely that nominal wages will increase in the short-run, when labor prices are sticky. Since nominal wages remain fixed but prices are rising, real wages are decreasing.

INCORRECT ANSWER

A negative supply shock will cause an increase in the price level. Although workers may desire a wage increase, it is unlikely that nominal wages will increase in the short-run, when labor prices are sticky.

So, if prices are rising but nominal wages are fixed, how are real wages affected?

43. CORRECT ANSWER: C

If no corrective action is taken, the economy will self-adjust to the long-run aggregate output. In this case, a recession, the high rate of unemployment will eventually cause nominal wages to decrease and short-run aggregate supply will shift to the right to restore long-run aggregate output.

INCORRECT ANSWER

In the short-run the economy is in recession. How will lingering unemployment affect nominal wages in the long-run?

44. CORRECT ANSWER: A

According to the graph, this economy is experiencing inflation. In its current state, the unemployment rate is below the natural rate but wages are sticky. In the long-run, nominal wages will become unstuck and will increase, which will shift the short-run aggregate supply curve to the left to restore long-run equilibrium.

INCORRECT ANSWER

According to the graph, this economy is experiencing inflation, with an unemployment rate that is below the natural rate. This is a recipe for rising wages—but not in the short-run.

TOPIC 3: POLICY MIX

DIFFICULTY LEVEL 2

45. CORRECT ANSWER: D

An expansionary monetary policy must be used to reduce interest rates and spur greater investment. However, this action will increase the price level so a contractionary fiscal policy must also be used maintain the price level.

INCORRECT ANSWER

Interest rates must be reduced to spur greater investment. How can this rate change be accomplished without increasing the price level?

46. CORRECT ANSWER: A

To correct severe inflation, it is necessary to decrease aggregate demand. An increase in taxes will decrease the aggregate demand and a decrease in the money supply would decrease it further.

INCORRECT ANSWER

A change in taxes and the money supply will only have a direct effect on aggregate demand. In which direction must aggregate demand shift to address inflation?

47. CORRECT ANSWER: E

An expansionary policy is needed to bring the economy out of recession. Increasing government spending is an expansionary fiscal policy and decreasing the discount rate is an expansionary monetary policy. Together, these policies will have an overall effect of increasing aggregate demand and ending the recession.

INCORRECT ANSWER

A pair of expansionary policies are needed to bring the economy out of recession. Be careful not to choose an answer that includes both a contractionary and expansionary policy, as they may cancel each other out.

48. CORRECT ANSWER: E

Eliminate any answer that includes a change in monetary policy, as the question requires only fiscal policy changes. Then, choose the answer that includes two expansionary fiscal policies—an increase in government spending and a decrease in taxes.

INCORRECT ANSWER

Start by eliminating any answer that includes a change in monetary policy, as the question requires only fiscal policy changes. Which combination of fiscal policies cause the greatest increase in aggregate demand?

49. CORRECT ANSWER: A

An increase in the money supply is needed to reduce interest rates and stimulate investment spending, but this policy will also increase real output. A contractionary fiscal policy is needed to counteract this expansionary monetary policy—such as a decrease in government spending.

INCORRECT ANSWER

Cross out any answer choice that does not include an increase in the money supply. An increase in the money supply is needed to reduce interest rates and stimulate investment spending, but this policy will also increase real output. Now what fiscal policy can counteract this expansionary monetary policy?

50. CORRECT ANSWER: C

An increase in government spending and a purchase of government bonds are both expansionary policies that will decrease unemployment and increase real gross domestic product. The bond purchases will also increase the money supply, which will cause a decrease in the interest rate. The only answer choice that includes a correct combination of effects is choice C.

INCORRECT ANSWER

The question lays out the policy choices for you. All that is left to do is summarize the effects and choose an answer that matches. Looking at the answer choices, you must determine the cumulative on real GDP, the interest rate, and unemployent. Keep in mind, only monetary policy has an effect on the interest rate.

51. CORRECT ANSWER: D

The correct answer must have both an expansionary fiscal and monetary policy or it must have both a contractionary fiscal and monetary policy. Choice D includes a tax increase (contractionary) and an increase in interest rates (contractionary), which means that Congress is reinforcing the Fed's policy. The other choices combine an expansionary and contractionary policy.

INCORRECT ANSWER

The four incorrect answers combine an expansionary policy and a contractionary policy. Look for the answer whose policies result in the same change in aggregate demand. It may help to jot notes in the margin too keep track of all the changes.

52. CORRECT ANSWER: D

To address a severe recession the government should enact expansionary fiscal and monetary policies. Among the choices, the only pair of expansionary policies is an increase in government transfers and an open market purchase of government bonds.

To address a severe recession the government should enact expansionary fiscal and monetary policies. Start narrowing down your answer by eliminating any choices with a pair of contractionary policies.

53. CORRECT ANSWER: B

The answer choices include three policy changes. Try not to be overwhelmed by all of the combinations—scribble notes in your test booklet to keep your thoughts organized and cross out answer choices that don't fit the criteria.

The answer most likely to result in an increase in aggregate demand will have three expansionary policies: an increase in government spending, a decrease in the reserve requirement, and an open-market operation that buys bonds.

54. CORRECT ANSWER: D

Most factors affect aggregate supply or aggregate demand exclusively. However, a decrease in business taxes would increase both aggregate supply and demand. Firms would produce more output if a decrease in taxes would increase their profits and firms would conduct more investment spending since the tax reduction leaves them with more disposable funds.

Most of the answer choices affect aggregate supply or aggregate demand exclusively. Which change would both increase profits and encourage more spending?

55. CORRECT ANSWER: D

With a combination of expansionary and contractionary policies, it is impossible to determine the net effect on gross domestic product without some quantatative information. It is also impossible to determine if a budget deficit will result, but it seems unlikely because a contractionary fiscal policy would definitely include an increase in taxes and/or a decrease in government spending (which moves the budget toward surplus).

The only certainty under these policies is that interest rates will decrease because the expansionary monetary policy will increase the money supply.

When contractionary and explansionary policies are combined, it is difficult to determine their net effect without some quantitative details, such as how much spending was increased or decreased. Since there is no such information provided by the question, what changes can you be certain about?

56. CORRECT ANSWER: D

A decrease in the money supply will cause an increase in the nominal interest rate. If this contractionary monetary policy is followed by an expansionary fiscal policy, the net effect on output is indeterminate without additional quantatative information.

A contractionary monetary policy will cause an increae in the nominal interest rate. What will be the effect on unemployment with a contradictory pair of policies?

57. CORRECT ANSWER: C

The best way to reduce unemployment is to use a combination of expansionary fiscal and monetary policies. Eliminate any answers that include contractionary policies, such as an increase in taxes, a decrease in government spending, selling bonds, increasing reserve requirements, or raising the discount rate.

INCORRECT ANSWER

The best way to reduce unemployment is to use a combination of expansionary fiscal and monetary policies. Eliminate any answers that include contractionary policies, such as an increase in taxes, a decrease in government spending, selling bonds, increasing reserve requirements, or raising the discount rate.

TOPIC 4: GOVERNMENT DEFICITS AND DEBT

DIFFICULTY LEVEL 2

58. CORRECT ANSWER: C

The government budget balance is calculated by subtracting the value of all government spending on goods and services and the value of government transfers from the amount of money received by the government from taxes.

INCORRECT ANSWER

The government budget balance is a calculation used to determine if the government's budget is balanced, in deficit, or in surplus. Consider from where the government gets its money, and how the money is used.

59. CORRECT ANSWER: D

A budget deficit occurs when a government spends and transfers more money than it receives in taxes. Be careful not to be fooled by a single department of government that spends more than it has been allocated. A deficit occurs when all of the government's spending and transfers exceed taxes.

INCORRECT ANSWER

A deficit indicates that there is not enough money to fund expenditures.

60. CORRECT ANSWER: B

An expansionary fiscal policy includes some or all of the following elements: an increase in government spending, an increase in government transfers, and a decrease in taxes. Any of these changes will move a government budget toward deficit, as the government will increase the money going out and decrease the money coming in.

INCORRECT ANSWER

Consider what an expansionary policy may include: an increase in government spending, an increase in government transfers, and a decrease in taxes. What effect will these changes have on the government's bank account?

61. CORRECT ANSWER: E

When the U.S. government spends more than it receives in taxes, it must borrow funds. However, the government does not apply for a bank loan. Rather, the U.S. Treasury issues new bonds. Purchases of the bonds provides the funds for government spending, and the bonds are repaid, with interest, by American taxpayers.

INCORRECT ANSWER

The government must borrow money to finance deficit spending, but it does not apply for a traditional loan or print money. From whom does the government acquire its needed funds?

62. CORRECT ANSWER: B

If the government is increasing its spending without an increase in taxes, it must increase its borrowing to fund the spending. The increase in borrowing will cause an increase in demand in the loanable funds market, resulting in an increase in interest rates.

How does government borrowing change when the government spends more without increasing taxes? What results from the change in borrowing?

63. CORRECT ANSWER: C

The national debt is the net result of past and current budget deficits and surpluses. An annual budget deficit will add to the debt while an annual budget surplus will decrease the debt. The debt is owed to the owners of U.S. Treasury bondholders, whoever they may be.

Consider that an annual budget deficit will add to the debt while an annual budget surplus will decrease the debt.

64. CORRECT ANSWER: E

Policymakers have created a contractionary fiscal policy. While it will move the budget balance toward surplus and possibly reduce the debt, it will also cause aggregate output to decrease, resulting in an increase in unemployment.

Policymakers have created a contractionary fiscal policy. While it will move the budget balance toward surplus and possibly reduce the debt, what other changes will result from this decrease in aggregate demand?

65. CORRECT ANSWER: A

A budget deficit occurs when government expenditures and transfers exceed tax revenues. The budget only reflects transactions conducted by the government.

The government budget only reflects transactions conducted by the government, not by banks, foreigners, or households.

66. CORRECT ANSWER: A

While the government could increase its income through other means, it typically issues bonds. The U.S. government funds deficit spending by issuing Treasury bonds and selling them to the public.

INCORRECT ANSWER

Some of the answers are possible methods the government could use to increase its income, but the correct answer is the means most commonly used.

67. CORRECT ANSWER: D

As the U.S. economy moves toward recession, tax receipts decrease (though tax rates remain unchanged) while government transfers increase, as more Americans qualify for welfare and unemployment assistance. As a result, the budget moves toward deficit.

INCORRECT ANSWER

Automatic stabilizers include government transfers like unemployment and welfare benefits and the progressive tax code, in which smaller tax payments are made as income declines. How would a recession affect the use of these stabilizers? What effect would these stabilizers have on the budget?

68. CORRECT ANSWER: B

An increase in the budget deficit means that the government will increase its demand for loanable funds, resulting in an increase in the real interest rate. As the real interest rate rises, investment spending declines.

INCORRECT ANSWER

An increase in the deficit means that the government must increase its borrowing. How will increased borrowing affect the real interest rate? How do changes in the real interest rate affect investment spending?

THE PHILLIPS CURVE

TOPIC 1: SHORT-RUN AND LONG-RUN PHILLIPS CURVES

DIFFICULTY LEVEL 2

1. CORRECT ANSWER: C

The short-run Phillips curve is a downward-sloping curve that represents the indirect relationship between the inflation rate and the unemployment rate.

INCORRECT ANSWER

The curve in the graph represents an indirect relationship between the inflation rate and the unemployment rate.

2. CORRECT ANSWER: A

The short-run Phillips curve portrays an indirect relationship between the inflation rate and the unemployment rate, meaning lower inflation rates are associated with higher unemployment rates.

INCORRECT ANSWER

The short-run Phillips curve portrays an indirect relationship between the inflation rate and the unemployment rate.

3. CORRECT ANSWER: C

The short-run Phillips curve portrays an indirect relationship between the inflation rate and the unemployment rate, meaning a high rate of inflation is associated with a low unemployment rate.

4. CORRECT ANSWER: D

An increase in aggregate demand will cause an increase in price level and a decrease in the unemployment rate. The only movement on the graph that represents these changes is a movement up along the SRPC1 curve from point Y to point X.

Shifts in aggregate demand translate to movements along the short-run Phillips curve, while shifts in short-run aggregate supply translate to shifts in the short-run Phillips curve.

INCORRECT ANSWER

Shifts in aggregate demand translate to movements along the short-run Phillips curve, while shifts in short-run aggregate supply translate to shifts in the short-run Phillips curve. In this scenario, an increase in aggregate demand causes price level to increase and the unemployment rate to decrease. How is that reflected on the SRPC?

5. **CORRECT ANSWER: A**

A contractionary monetary policy will cause a decrease in aggregate demand, a decrease in price level, and an increase in the unemployment rate. It is represented as a movement down along the short-run Phillips curve.

Shifts in aggregate demand translate to movements along the short-run Phillips curve, while shifts in short-run aggregate supply translate to shifts in the short-run Phillips curve.

INCORRECT ANSWER

A contractionary monetary policy causes a decrease in aggregate supply. How will the price level and unemployment rate be affected?

Shifts in aggregate demand translate to movements along the short-run Phillips curve, while shifts in short-run aggregate supply translate to shifts in the short-run Phillips curve.

6. **CORRECT ANSWER: C**

A decrease in the price of oil will cause an increase in short-run aggregate supply, resulting in a decrease in price level and a decrease in the unemployment rate. This change is represented by a leftward shift of the short-run Phillips curve.

Think of the short-run Phillips curve as a mirror image of the short-run aggregate supply curve. Anything that shifts SRAS to the right, such as a decrease in input prices, will shift the SRPC to the left.

INCORRECT ANSWER

A leftward shift of the short-run Phillips curve indicates that both the inflation rate and the unemployment rate are falling. What change in the economy can cause these results?

7. **CORRECT ANSWER: B**

In the short-run, the Phillips curve shows the trade off between the inflation rate and the unemployment rate. In the long-run, there is no trade-off between inflation and unemployment, as an economy will always produce at its full-employment level of output in the long-run.

INCORRECT ANSWER

The Phillips curve is closely related to the AD-AS model. In the short-run, a change in aggregate demand will cause opposite changes in price level and unemployment. In the long-run, the only change that remains is in price level. How is that reflected in the SRPC and LRPC?

8. **CORRECT ANSWER: D**

A movement up along the SRPC reflects the increase in inflation and decrease in the unemployment rate. Such a movement is caused by an increase in aggregate demand, which can occur when exports increase.

INCORRECT ANSWER

The changes described in the question are indicated by a movement up along the SRPC, which can be caused by an increase in aggregate demand.

9. **CORRECT ANSWER: D**

The long-run Phillips curve is vertical at the natural rate of unemployment, reflecting the idea that in the long-run, aggregate output is unrelated to price level.

INCORRECT ANSWER

The long-run Phillips curve reflects the principle that aggregate output is unrelated to price level in the long-run.

10. **CORRECT ANSWER: C**

An increase in nominal wages will cause an increase in price level and unemployment in the short-run. In the long-run, the economy will self-correct and return to full employment. These changes are reflected by a rightward shift in the short-run Phillips curve but there will be no change in the long-run Phillips curve.

INCORRECT ANSWER

Think of the short-run Phillips curve as a mirror image of the short-run aggregate supply curve. Anything that shifts SRAS to the left, such as an increase in nominal wages, will shift the SRPC to the right. How will the long-run Phillips curve be affected?

11. CORRECT ANSWER: D

Think of the long-run Phillips curve as a mirror image of long-run aggregate supply. If the economy is currently producing at an unemployment rate that is greater than that at the LRPC, then unemployment is greater than the natural rate, indicating that the economy is in recession.

INCORRECT ANSWER

Think of the long-run Phillips curve as a mirror image of long-run aggregate supply. If current output results in an unemployment rate that is greater than that at the LRPC, what is indicated about the state of the economy?

12. CORRECT ANSWER: B

In the long-run, this economy will self-correct its recession and return to full-employment output. The recession will cause nominal wages to decrease in the long-run, short-run aggregate supply will increase, the short-run Phillips curve will shift to the left, and the unemployment rate will decrease back to the natural rate of unemployment.

INCORRECT ANSWER

This economy is currently in recession, but the macroeconomy will self-correct a recession in the long-run.

13. CORRECT ANSWER: C

The natural rate of unemployment is equal to the unemployment rate at the long-run Phillips curve. It represents the unemployment rate at the full-employment level of output, or potential output. In the long-run, the economy will always return to this level of output.

INCORRECT ANSWER

It is helpful to think of the long-run Phillips curve as a mirror image of long-run aggregate supply.

14. CORRECT ANSWER: D

An unemployment rate of 4 percent is to the left of the long-run Phillips curve. The LRPC represents the non-accelerating inflation rate of unemployment (NAIRU), meaning that any unemployment rate below NAIRU, which is 5% in the graph, will cause the inflation rate to increase.

Another way to consider this question is to picture the mirror image of this graph in the AD-AS model, which would portray an inflationary gap. In the long-run, an inflationary gap is closed when SRAS shifts to the left, resulting in an increase in price level.

INCORRECT ANSWER

The long-run Phillips curve represents the non-accelerating inflation rate of unemployment (NAIRU). What will result if the current unemployment rate is below NAIRU?

15. CORRECT ANSWER: B

The movement from Point A to Point B indicates a decrease in the unemployment rate and an increase in the inflation rate, which are the results of an increase in aggregate demand. The increase in military expenditures is the only choice that fits these criteria.

INCORRECT ANSWER

The movement from Point A to Point B indicates a decrease in the unemployment rate and an increase in the inflation rate, which are the results of an increase in aggregate demand.

Narrow down the correct answer by crossing out any changes that only affect aggregate supply.

TOPIC 2: DEMAND-PULL VERSUS COST-PUSH INFLATION

DIFFICULTY LEVEL 2

16. CORRECT ANSWER: C

Demand-pull inflation occurs when there is an increase in aggregate demand. Graph a rightward shift in AD and trace the effect on price level to see for yourself.

INCORRECT ANSWER

Draw an AD-AS graph to help determine the cause of an increase in price level. Which shift is likely called demand-pull?

17. CORRECT ANSWER: D

Demand-pull inflation is caused by an increase in aggregate demand, so the initial shift moves equilibrium from point C to point X. In the long-run, the demand-pull inflation will cause nominal wages to rise and short-run aggregate supply will shift left, moving equilibrium from point X to point Y.

INCORRECT ANSWER

Demand-pull inflation is caused by an increase in aggregate demand. What results from this shift in the long-run?

18. **CORRECT ANSWER: C**

Demand-pull inflation is caused by an increase in aggregate demand. Among the choices, only a decrease in the real interest rate would cause this change, as interest-sensitive investment and consumption spending will increase.

INCORRECT ANSWER

Demand-pull inflation is caused by an increase in aggregate demand.

19. **CORRECT ANSWER: E**

Cost-push inflation is caused by a negative supply shock.

INCORRECT ANSWER

Same as above.

20. **CORRECT ANSWER: B**

The government must use a contractionary policy to decrease aggregate demand, which will result in an increase in the unemployment rate.

INCORRECT ANSWER

The government must use a contractionary policy to decrease aggregate demand.

21. **CORRECT ANSWER: D**

Cost-push inflation is caused by a decrease in short-run aggregate supply. An increase in nominal wages would cause this shift.

INCORRECT ANSWER

Cost-push inflation is caused by a decrease in short-run aggregate supply.

TOPIC 3: ROLE OF EXPECTATIONS

22. CORRECT ANSWER: E

If there is an increase in the expected rate of inflation, households will immediately demand an increase in nominal wages, causing a decline in short-run aggregate supply and a rightward shift of the short-run Phillips curve.

INCORRECT ANSWER

Changes in inflationary expectations cause an immediate shift in short-run aggregate supply, as households and firms adjust their demands for nominal wages.

23. CORRECT ANSWER: B

A rightward shift of the short-run Phillips curve indicates an increase in both the unemployment rate and the inflation rate. Such a change could be the result of an increase in inflationary expectations resulting in households immediately demanding an increase in nominal wages.

INCORRECT ANSWER

A rightward shift of the short-run Phillips curve indicates an increase in both the unemployment rate and the inflation rate.

24. CORRECT ANSWER: E

A decrease in the money supply is an expansionary policy that will result in a decrease in price level. If people are aware of the decrease in money supply, they will rationally expect prices to fall.

INCORRECT ANSWER

Assume that people will respond rationally to changes in the economy. Therefore a decrease in inflationary expectations will be caused by a change that will likely decrease the price level.

25. CORRECT ANSWER: A

Rational expectations suggests that people base their expectations about the future on all available information, including historical data and knowledge of policy changes.

INCORRECT ANSWER

As the term suggests, people use logic and reason to form rational expectations about the future inflation rate.

26. **CORRECT ANSWER: D**

An increase in inflation and unemployment is caused by a decrease in short-run aggregate supply. SRAS decreases when there is an increase in production costs, such as an increase in nominal wages. If workers increase their inflationary expectations, they will immediately demand an increase in nominal wages.

INCORRECT ANSWER

An increase in inflation and unemployment is caused by a decrease in short-run aggregate supply.

27. **CORRECT ANSWER: C**

Rational expectations theory says that households and firms base their decisions regarding wages mainly on their expectations of future economic conditions. If they expect higher prices in the future, they quickly demand higher wages.

INCORRECT ANSWER

Workers are basing their demand for higher wages on a reasonable expectation of future price increases.

28. **CORRECT ANSWER: C**

When households and firms behave according to rational expectations, an expansionary policy will immediately cause workers to demand an increase to nominal wages, as they will want to maintain their real wages. While prices will rise, causing an increase in nominal GDP, real GDP will remain unchanged.

INCORRECT ANSWER

An expansionary policy will cause prices to increase, but rational expectations theory contends that workers will demand an immediate increase in nominal wages. How will nominal and real output be affected by these changes?

29. **CORRECT ANSWER: B**

If an expansionary policy is anticipated, households and firms will behave accordingly. The policy will increase price level and workers will immediately demand an increase in nominal wages. While real output will be unchanged, the increase in price level will cause an increase in nominal GDP.

INCORRECT ANSWER

If an expansionary policy is anticipated, households and firms will behave accordingly. The policy will increase price level and workers will immediately demand an increase in nominal wages.

Stabilization Policies

Economic Growth

DEFINITION OF ECONOMIC GROWTH

DIFFICULTY LEVEL 2

1. **CORRECT ANSWER: B**

    Real gross domestic product per capita measures the aggregate output of an economy, controlling for changes in price level and the size of the population.

    INCORRECT ANSWER

    A country's standard of living indicates the level of wealth, comfort, material goods, and necessities available to the average person.

2. **CORRECT ANSWER: C**

    If real GDP is growing at a faster rate than the population, then real GDP per person, or per capita, must be increasing.

    INCORRECT ANSWER

    If real GDP is growing at a faster rate than the population then which of the answer choices is necessarily true?

3. **CORRECT ANSWER: C**

    The best definition of economic growth is a sustained increase in real output, not merely a short-run increase. While output may ebb and flow in the short-term, the true sign of growth is an increase in output in the long-run.

    INCORRECT ANSWER

    A simple increase in output or aggregate supply does not necessarily indicate economic growth.

4. **CORRECT ANSWER: B**

    Long-run economic growth is a sustained increase in real output, indicated by an increase in aggregate supply.

While an increase in real GDP per capita is a good indicator of economic growth, national income is not necessarily shared among all citizens. These broad measurements estimate that economic conditions are improving in the country, but they are not a guarantee that the average citizen is experiencing an improvement in standard of living.

INCORRECT ANSWER

Economic growth is a sustained increase in real output. This definition estimates that economic conditions are improving, but how strong can this prediction be?

5. **CORRECT ANSWER: B**

An outward shift of the production possibilities curve indicates an increase in the potential output of an economy, i.e. economic growth.

INCORRECT ANSWER

The shift indicated by this graph shows that this economy can produce more capital and consumer goods than before. What is indicated by such a shift in potential output?

6. **CORRECT ANSWER: C**

Economic growth is represented by an increase in output in the long-run. A rightward shift of long-run aggregate supply indicates that the potential output of the economy has increased.

INCORRECT ANSWER

Is economic growth a short-run or long-run change?

7. **CORRECT ANSWER: C**

Questions about an economy's standard of living often refer to real output per capita. If an economy is said to be producing more output per person, then the standard of living is improving. Answer choice C indicates an improvement in standard of living because, although output is declining, the population size is declining more. The net result of these changes is that there is more aggregate output per person.

INCORRECT ANSWER

The answer choices indicate an array of changes. Focus on the pertinent details—an economy's standard of living is best measured by real output per capita.

8. **CORRECT ANSWER: B**

A righward shift of long-run aggregate supply indicates that potential output has increased. There are many ways to indicate this change, e.g., an increase in full-employment output, economic growth, an increase in production possibilities.

INCORRECT ANSWER

The graph indicates an increase in the long-run aggregate supply, or an increase in long-run output.

9. **CORRECT ANSWER: E**

Economic growth is indicated by increases in long-run aggregate supply and production possibilities because these shifts represent a sustained increase in output.

INCORRECT ANSWER

Remember that economic growth is a sustained increase in output.

DETERMINANTS OF ECONOMIC GROWTH

TOPIC 1: INVESTMENT IN HUMAN CAPITAL

TOPIC 2: INVESTMENT IN PHYSICAL CAPITAL

TOPIC 3: RESEARCH AND DEVELOPMENT AND TECHNOLOGICAL PROGRESS

DIFFICULTY LEVEL 2

1. CORRECT ANSWER: B

An increase in the educational attainment of the population represents an increase in human capital. A more educated population will likely result in more productive workers and increased potential output.

INCORRECT ANSWER

Economic growth is usually the result of increased worker productivity.

2. CORRECT ANSWER: D

An increase in population will likely result in an increase in the size of the labor force. By increasing the pool of workers, the production possibilities of the economy can increase.

INCORRECT ANSWER

Another way to state this question is, "An increase in which of the following will increase the production possibilities of the economy?"

3. CORRECT ANSWER: E

The main factors that affect economic growth are changes in the size and productivity of the labor force, physical capital, and the degree of technology available. If these factors improve, the economy will become more productive and its potential output will increase.

INCORRECT ANSWER

In order to produce goods and services an economy needs natural resources, labor, physical capital, and human capital. If any of these change, the potential output of the economy can change.

4. **CORRECT ANSWER: B**

Human capital refers to the knowledge and training possessed by workers. Were there an increase in financial aid for college students, the population would likely become more educated and become more productive workers.

INCORRECT ANSWER

Human capital refers to the knowledge and training possessed by workers.

5. **CORRECT ANSWER: C**

By replacing simpler production machinery with technologically advanced production tools represents investment spending on capital goods and technology.

INCORRECT ANSWER

The question implies that this machinery will be used to produce other goods or services.

6. **CORRECT ANSWER: D**

Productivity measures the amount of output produced by a unit of labor. Productivity is affected by technology, production methods, and the quality and quantity of labor and physical capital.

INCORRECT ANSWER

Productivity measures the amount of output produced by a unit of labor.

7. **CORRECT ANSWER: A**

Capital represents the amount of productive tools or machinery available to workers for producing goods and services. With more capital, workers can produce more output per unit of time. In fact, output per worker per unit of time is the definition of productivity. If both of these factors increase, economic growth increases.

INCORRECT ANSWER

Capital represents the amount of productive tools or machinery available to workers for producing goods and services.

8. **CORRECT ANSWER: D**

Technological progress improves physical capital, improves production methods, and creates new industries, all of which lead to economic growth.

INCORRECT ANSWER

Economic growth is a sustained increase in real output. Which of the choices result in an economy increasing how much it can potentially produce?

GROWTH POLICY

DIFFICULTY LEVEL 2

1. CORRECT ANSWER: C

Economic growth occurs when investments spending on capital goods or human capital increases. If there were an increase in tax incentives to encourage investment spending then the economy would likely grow.

INCORRECT ANSWER

To cause economic growth, there must be an improvement in the potential output of an economy. This increase in potential is usually caused by an increase in physical and human capital.

2. CORRECT ANSWER: D

While Point A is an attainable level of production and will lead to the greatest economic growth in the future, it is not necessarily the best level of production for this economy. It is impossible to determine the best level of production from a production possibilities graph, as it only displays what an economy can produce, not what it should produce.

INCORRECT ANSWER

Point A will result in the greatest economic growth, as it is an attainable level of production that produces the most capital goods (which can then be used for further production). Is Point A the best level of production for this economy?

3. CORRECT ANSWER: E

If government supports investment spending by firms by offering increased subsidies then firms will increase their purchases of productive capital and potential output will increase.

INCORRECT ANSWER

To help an economy grow, the government must support the measures that cause potential output to increase.

4. **CORRECT ANSWER: A**

An increase in national savings will increase the supply of loanable funds, resulting in a decrease in real interest rates. This rate decrease will encourage borrowing and investment spending among firms and an increase in economic growth.

INCORRECT ANSWER

Consider how an increase in national savings will affect the loanable funds market. How will changes in that market affect investment spending and economic growth?

5. **CORRECT ANSWER: B**

If the national government conducts deficit spending, it means that it is funding its spending through increased borrowing, causing an increase in the demand for loanable funds. This policy would result in an increase in real interest rates, which will decrease investment spending by private firms who will now find borrowing to be too expensive. This process is referred to as "crowding out."

INCORRECT ANSWER

Deficit spending is when a government spends more money in a given time period than it takes in through taxes. Governments must increase their borrowing to conduct deficit spending. How will this borrowing affect the loanable funds market?

6. **CORRECT ANSWER: E**

The economy is in recession, so an expansionary policy is needed to increase aggregate demand and equilibrium output. However, when in recession, an expansionary fiscal policy will increase deficit spending and raise real interest rates, which can decrease the level of investment spending and economic growth. Though a contractionary policy can decrease real interest rates and encourage investment spending, it would worsen the recession. Its best to leave the fiscal policy unchanged.

An expansionary monetary policy will increase aggregate demand while also decreasing real interest rates, so it presents a perfect solution. Buying bonds will achieve the expansionary monetary policy.

INCORRECT ANSWER

To solve a recession while still encouraging investment spending, policymakers must increase aggregate demand while decreasing real interest rates. What combination of policies will achieve this net effect?

CORRECT ANSWER: B

An increase in the government deficit will cause "crowding out," which is a decrease in private investment spending resulting from the increase in demand for loanable funds. The government's borrowing causes an increase in the real interest rate, which decreases private investment spending and slows economic growth.

INCORRECT ANSWER

Economic growth is driven by investment spending on improvements in technology, physical capital, and human capital. Which answer choice would be an obstacle to investment spending?

Open Economy: International Trade and Finance

BALANCE OF PAYMENTS ACCOUNTS

TOPIC 1: BALANCE OF TRADE

DIFFICULTY LEVEL 2

1. **CORRECT ANSWER: B**

   When more exports are sold than imports are purchased, then an economy has a trade surplus. In other words, the value of this economy's net exports is positive.

   INCORRECT ANSWER

   Since this economy is exporting more than it is importing, the value of its net exports is positive.

2. **CORRECT ANSWER: B**

   The trade deficit concerns only the value of goods and services imported and exported from an economy. When U.S. firms purchase goods from Japan, the value of imports to the U.S. economy increases, moving the trade balance toward deficit.

   Be careful not to choose D. Although a depreciation of the U.S. dollar may be caused by a trade deficit, this depreciation could also be caused by a change in capital flows, which does not directly concern the trade balane.

   INCORRECT ANSWER

   The trade deficit grows when exports decrease or imports decrease.

3. **CORRECT ANSWER: C**

   Since net exports are increasing (moving toward a positive value, or surplus), aggregate demand is increasing, which results in an increase in equilibrium income.

INCORRECT ANSWER

The value of imports is decreasing, which moves moves net exports toward a positive value. This change will also increase aggregate demand. How do these changes affect the trade balance and equilibrium income?

4. **CORRECT ANSWER: B**

An economy's trade balance moves toward deficit when its imports increase and its exports decrease. The value of its net exports moves toward negative.

INCORRECT ANSWER

An increased deficit in the balance of trade means the value of imports is rising and the value of exports is declining.

5. **CORRECT ANSWER: B**

The U.S. trade deficit will decrease if its exports increase and/or its imports decrease. For this outcome to occur, the value of the U.S. dollar must depreciate relative to other currencies (i.e., other currencies appreciate relative to the dollar). The trade deficit would then decrease because U.S. goods and services would feel relatively inexpensive to foreign buyers.

INCORRECT ANSWER

For the U.S. trade deficit to decrease, U.S. goods and services need to become a more attractive purchase to foreign buyers.

TOPIC 2: CURRENT ACCOUNT

DIFFICULTY LEVEL 2

6. **CORRECT ANSWER: C**

The current account measures the flow of goods, services, and income from one nation to another. Current account payments create no liability for future payments. The payment from the South Korean manufacturer to the U.S. shipping company represents a payment for services rendered by another economy. This payment creates no liability for future payments between these two firms. This would be counted as a credit in the U.S. current acccount and a debit in the South Korean current account.

INCORRECT ANSWER

The current account measures the flow of goods, services, and income from one nation to another.

7. **CORRECT ANSWER: E**

The purchase of the lumber company by a Swedish firm represents the purchase of a physical asset in the United States, so it is counted in the financial account. This purchase creates a liability for the future—profits from the lumber company will be paid to the Swedish firm in the future. The other choices represent transactions that do not involve liabilities for the future—they are "one and done" transactions.

INCORRECT ANSWER

Current account transactions do not involve future liabilities—they are "one and done" transactions. In other words, current account transactions do not create the necessity for future transactions.

8. **CORRECT ANSWER: D**

The current account includes transactions that do not create future liability, including the purchase of goods and a payment of profits. These payments are not required to recur in the future. The purchase of stock in a foreign corporation creates a liability for the stock-issuing corporation, who owes the stockholder shares of profits or assets in the future.

INCORRECT ANSWER

It is misleading to assume that the current account transactions only include payments for goods and services. The current account includes any transactions that do not create future liabilities, such as one-time transfers of funds.

9. **CORRECT ANSWER: D**

A current account deficit is also known as a trade deficit, which means this country has made more payments for goods, services, income, and transfers to the rest of the world than it has received from abroad for the same reasons. The money to pay for these current account transactions must have an origin, so they must be from a surplus in the financial account from payments by foreigners for domestic assets.

INCORRECT ANSWER

According to the balance of payments model, the current account and the financial account must balance.

TOPIC 3: FINANCIAL ACCOUNT

DIFFICULTY LEVEL 2

10. CORRECT ANSWER: C

Foreign direct investment involves the purchase of factors of production in another economy for use in that economy. Examples of direct foreign investment usually include a the purchase of a factory in the domestic economy by a foreign firm, such as when Volkswagen (a German company) constructed an auto factory in the United States. Such transactions are counted in the financial account.

INCORRECT ANSWER

Be sure to distinguish between the purchase of financial assets in a foreign economy from making direct investment purchases of capital goods.

11. CORRECT ANSWER: A

The purchase of foreign financial assets by Chinese investors represents a debit from China's financial account.

Incorrect answer: Is China buying an asset from the French corporation or goods and services? These different types of purchases would be categorized differently in China's balance of payments account.

12. CORRECT ANSWER: A

The American company's purchase of productive capital in Indonesia is represented in the financial account because the transaction creates a future liability. The manufacturing plant will owe its output and profits to the American firm and the American firm will owe wages to the workers in Indonesia.

INCORRECT ANSWER

Transactions that create future liabilities are included in the financial account while those that do not are included in the current account. Imports and the balance of trade concern purchases of final goods and services.

FOREIGN EXCHANGE MARKET

TOPIC 1: DEMAND FOR AND SUPPLY OF FOREIGN EXCHANGE

DIFFICULTY LEVEL 2

1. CORRECT ANSWER: B

A decrease in import restrictions from China will encourage Americans to purchase Chinese goods and services. Americans will supply more dollars to the foreign exchange market and demand more Chinese yuan. This will cause the U.S. dollar to depreciate and the Chinese yuan to appreciate in value.

2. CORRECT ANSWER: B

The graph is showing a rightward shift in demand, which means that the quantity of U.S. dollars demanded at various exchange rates is increasing, i.e., demand for the U.S. dollar is increasing.

If there is confusion as to whether the graph represents U.S. dollars or euros, refer to the label on the horizontal axis for clarification.

INCORRECT ANSWER

It looks like demand is shifting to the right, but which currency does it represent? Refer to the label on the horizontal axis for clarification.

3. CORRECT ANSWER: E

The shift of demand represented by the graph occurs when Europeans increase their demand for the U.S. dollar. Such a shift occurs when Europeans hope to make purchases or investments in the United States. If U.S. interest rates are higher than European interest rates, then Europeans will increase their demand for U.S. dollars so they can purchase American financial assets.

INCORRECT ANSWER

Be sure to understand the shift before searching for the correct answer. Europeans are increasing their demand for the U.S. dollar

4. **CORRECT ANSWER: C**

American companies who purchase capital goods in India must supply more U.S. dollars to the foreign exchange market to purchase more Indian rupees. Since the question gives no indication of an increase in Indian demand for American products or assets, there is no change in demand for U.S. dollars.

INCORRECT ANSWER

A nation must supply its own currency to increase purchases in another nation.

5. **CORRECT ANSWER: E**

One must obtain U.S. dollars to purchase U.S. financial assets, so the demand for U.S. dollars will increase. Since the question offers no indication that Americans are trying to purchase more foreign products or assets, the supply of U.S. dollars in the foreign exchange market remains unchanged.

INCORRECT ANSWER

One must obtain U.S. dollars to purchase U.S. financial assets.

6. **CORRECT ANSWER: C**

American tourists will increase their purchases of goods and services in Brazil, such as hotel stays, food, and entertainment. For these purchases they will supply more U.S. dollars to the foreign exchange market and demand more Brazilian real.

7. **CORRECT ANSWER: B**

If inflation is lower in the United States, Russians will demand more American goods as they will be relatively cheaper to purchase. To purchase American goods, Russians will supply more rubles and demand more U.S. dollars.

INCORRECT ANSWER

Approach questions about international trade with the assumption, unless otherwise noted, that the nations referenced may trade freely. If there were free trade, people purchase goods and services where the prices are lowest. In this case, Russians will purchase goods and services from the United States.

8. **CORRECT ANSWER: D**

When incomes rise, consumers increase their demand for imports. If incomes are rising in Britain relative to the U.S. then British citizens will increase their demand for U.S. goods and services. British citizens will increase their the demand for U.S. dollars and increase the supply of British pounds, which are used to purchase dollars on the foreign exchange market.

INCORRECT ANSWER

When incomes rise, consumers tend to consume more imports.

TOPIC 2: EXCHANGE RATE DETERMINATION

DIFFICULTY LEVEL 1

9. CORRECT ANSWER: D

The exchange rate is refers to the amount of one nation's currency that must be supplied to purchase a unit of another nation's currency on the foreign exchange market.

INCORRECT ANSWER

There are many markets studied in macroeconomics and each one expresses its price with a different term. Purchases of another nation's currency occur on the foreign exchange market. What term does this market use to represent price?

DIFFICULTY LEVEL 2

10. CORRECT ANSWER: D

An increase in investment spending in India by U.S. firms will require those firms to supply American dollars in order to purchase Indian rupees. The increase in the supply of U.S. dollars will shift that curve to the right, resulting in a decrease in the exchange rate of rupees per dollar. In other words, the rupee will appreciate in value and the dollar will depreciate.

INCORRECT ANSWER

To conduct investment spending in India, U.S. firms will need to first purchase Indian rupees with U.S. dollars.

11. CORRECT ANSWER: D

One must obtain U.S. dollars to purchase U.S. financial assets, so the demand for U.S. dollars will increase. As demand increases for U.S. dollars increases, the equilibrium exchange rate for U.S. dollars increases, making the U.S. dollar appreciate in value relative to foreign currencies.

INCORRECT ANSWER

One must obtain U.S. dollars to purchase U.S. financial assets. How will an increase in purchases of U.S. assets affect the value of the dollar?

12. CORRECT ANSWER: A

An increase in exports from the United States indicates that foreign nations are purchasing more U.S. goods and services. In order to do this, foreigners must demand more U.S. dollars and supply more of their own currencies. These exchanges will result in an increase in the value of the U.S. dollar relative to foreign currencies.

INCORRECT ANSWER

An increase in exports from the United States indicates that foreign nations are purchasing more U.S. goods and services. What will foreigners need to do to make these purchases?

13. CORRECT ANSWER: B

As the inflation rate increases in Venezuela relative to that of its trading partners, its products and assets will rise in cost and foreigners will decrease their demand for them, resulting in a decrease in demand for the Venezuelan bolivar. As a result of declining demand for the Venezuelan bolivar, the currency will depreciate in value.

INCORRECT ANSWER

At higher prices, Venezuela's trading partners will increasingly find Venezuelan products and assets to be too expensive. How will this situation affect the Venezuelan bolivar in the foreign exchange market?

14. CORRECT ANSWER: B

A depreciation of the Mexican peso will occur if there is a decrease in demand for Mexican products and assets among its trading partners or an increase in Mexicans' demand for products and assets of its trading partners.

If Mexico's trading partners place a tariff on goods exported by Mexico, then those partners will decrease their demand for Mexican goods and the Mexican peso. This will result in a depreciation of the peso.

INCORRECT ANSWER

A depreciation of the Mexican peso will occur if there is a decrease in demand for Mexican products and assets among its trading partners or an increase in Mexicans' demand for products and assets of its trading partners.

15. CORRECT ANSWER: B

An increase in value, or appreciation, of the U.S. dollar occurs when there is an increase in the demand for the U.S. dollar or a decrease in the supply of the U.S. dollar on the foreign exchange market. If Americans begin to prefer U.S.-made goods to foreign-made goods, they will supply fewer dollars to the foreign exchange market, resulting in an appreciation in the U.S. dollar.

INCORRECT ANSWER

An increase in value, or appreciation, of the U.S. dollar occurs when there is an increase in the demand for the U.S. dollar or a decrease in the supply of the U.S. dollar on the foreign exchange market.

16. CORRECT ANSWER: E

To achieve an equilibrium exchange rate at X2 in the graph, demand for U.S. dollars must increase or supply of U.S. dollars must decrease. If financial assets in the U.S. increase relative to those in Europe, European investors will increase their demand for U.S. assets and increase their demand for the U.S. dollar to make those purchases.

INCORRECT ANSWER

To achieve an equilibrium exchange rate at X2 in the graph, demand for U.S. dollars must increase or supply of U.S. dollars must decrease.

TOPIC 3: CURRENCY APPRECIATION AND DEPRECIATION

DIFFICULTY LEVEL 2

17. CORRECT ANSWER: B

An increase in the value of the U.S. dollar increases its buying power in other economies, which benefits Americans hoping to purchase foreign products and assets.

However, it weakens the buying power of people holding foreign currency who hope to purchase products and assets in the United States.

INCORRECT ANSWER

An increase in the value of the U.S. dollar increases its buying power in foreign economies while weakening the buying power of foreign currencies in the U.S.

18. CORRECT ANSWER: B

If there are decreased real interest rates in the nation compared to the rest of the world, demand for the nation's currency will decrease and the supply of the nation's currency will increase. These shifts occur because investors will increase purchases of foreign financial assets to take advantage of the relatively higher real interest rates abroad.

INCORRECT ANSWER

A depreciation of a nation's currency occurs when demand for its currency decreases or the supply of its currency increases.

19. CORRECT ANSWER: B

For the country's currency to appreciate, it must be demanded more or supplied less. If foreign investors speculate that the currency will rise in value, they will likely increase purchases of the currency and cause it to increase in value.

INCORRECT ANSWER

The value of a country's currency will appreciate if it is demanded more or supplied less.

20. CORRECT ANSWER: B

If the price level in Canada has been rising faster than in the United States, Canadians will increasingly purchase products and assets from the United States and Americans will decrease their demand for Canadian products and assets. As a result, demand for the U.S. dollar will increase and the supply of the U.S. dollar will decrese, causing an appreciation of that currency.

INCORRECT ANSWER

According to the question, Canada's products and assets are becoming more expensive, so Canadians and Americans will likely buy American.

21. CORRECT ANSWER: D

An increase in U.S. household income would increase spending by Americans, including spending on Mexican products. This increase in demand for Mexico's exports will increase the demand for Mexico's peso, resulting in its appreciation in value.

INCORRECT ANSWER

Which answer choice causes an increase in demand for the peso or a decrease in supply of the peso?

22. CORRECT ANSWER: A

When the United States dollar depreciates in value, it is a benefit to American sellers of products and assets to customers abroad because foreign currencies appreciate in value and carry more buying power in the U.S.

INCORRECT ANSWER

If the U.S. dollar depreciates in value then foreign curriencies appreciate in value.

23. CORRECT ANSWER: B

If Chinese firms and citizens are increasing investments in the U.S., they are increasing their purchases of American assets. To purchase these assets, Chinese yuan are supplied and U.S. dollars are demanded, which depreciates the value of the yuan (a decrease in the dollar price of the yuan).

INCORRECT ANSWER

If Chinese firms and citizens are increasing investments in the U.S., they are increasing their purchases of American assets.

24. CORRECT ANSWER: C

If the dollar depreciates relative to the euro, then United States products and assets are becoming relatively cheaper to Europeans.

INCORRECT ANSWER

If the dollar depreciates relative to the euro, then United States products and assets are becoming relatively cheaper to Europeans.

IMPORTS, EXPORTS, AND FINANCIAL CAPITAL FLOWS

DIFFICULTY LEVEL 2

1. CORRECT ANSWER: D

As the United States' real interest increases relative to that of the rest of the world, the U.S. increasingly becomes a more attractive economy in which to make financial investments. Savers in the rest of the world will send their loanable funds to the United States.

INCORRECT ANSWER

Savers will usually invest their financial capital in the nation with the greatest rate of return.

2. CORRECT ANSWER: B

Since the real interest rate in the U.S. is decreasing relative to that of China, savers in the U.S. will increase their demand for Chinese financial assets. Capital will flow out of the U.S. and toward China, resulting in a depreciation of the U.S. dollar.

INCORRECT ANSWER

Capital flows toward the economy with the highest relative real interest rate.

3. CORRECT ANSWER: A

When the U.S. dollar appreciates in value, imports from foreign economies become relatively cheaper for Americans.

INCORRECT ANSWER

When the U.S. dollar appreciates, it is able to purchase more units of a foreign currency.

4. CORRECT ANSWER: C

As capital outflows from the United States increase, the supply of U.S. dollars on the foreign exchange market increases, resulting in a depreciation of the value of the dollar. Foreign consumers will now find that American goods and services are relatively cheaper and Americans will find foreign imports relatively more expensive, so the net exports of the U.S. will increase. The ultimate result is an increase in aggregate demand for the U.S. economy.

INCORRECT ANSWER

This question is solved by recognizing a rather extensive chain of events that begins with the increase in capital outflows from the United States, which causes the United States dollar to depreciate in value.

5. **CORRECT ANSWER: D**

A contractionary monetary policy will increase real interest rates in the United States, resulting in an increase in capital inflows and an appreciation of the U.S. Dollar. When the dollar appreciates, imports are relatively cheaper for Americans and American exports are relatively more expensive for foreigners, so imports increase and exports decrease.

INCORRECT ANSWER

A contractionary monetary policy will increase real interest rates in the United States, resulting in an increase in capital inflows.

6. **CORRECT ANSWER: A**

Japanese consumers must purchase U.S. dollars to purchase U.S. financial assets, so the supply of Japanese yen on the foreign exchange will increase and the demand for U.S. dollars will increase, resulting in an appreciation of the U.S. dollar. As a result of this appreciation, American consumers will increase their purchases of Japanese products, so Japanese net exports will increase.

INCORRECT ANSWER

Consider that Japanese consumers must first purchase U.S. dollars to purchase American financial assets. They must supply Japanese yen to purchase U.S. dollars, a transaction that will affect the value of the U.S. dollar.

7. **CORRECT ANSWER: B**

A decrease in interest rates in the United States makes the U.S. a less attractive economy in which to purchase financial assets, as the rate of return on these investments has decreased. As a result, capital inflows to the United States will decrease in the short-run.

INCORRECT ANSWER

Try not to be distracted by the mechanics of the Fed's policy. The important information in the question is that interest rates are decreasing.

8. CORRECT ANSWER: C

As the supply of loanable funds increases in Mexico, the real interest rate decreases, resulting in a decrease in demand for Mexican financial assets and a decrease in demand for the peso. The peso will depreciate and Mexican exports will be relatively less expensive, so exports will increase.

INCORRECT ANSWER

This question requires you to understand a chain reaction of changes. It begins with an increase in supply in the loanable funds market, which decreases the real interest rate in Mexico. How will this affect capital flows and the value of the peso?

RELATIONSHIPS BETWEEN INTERNATIONAL AND DOMESTIC FINANCIAL AND GOODS MARKETS

DIFFICULTY LEVEL 2

1. **CORRECT ANSWER: A**

   When the U.S. dollar appreciates in value, imports from foreign economies become relatively cheaper for Americans.

   INCORRECT ANSWER

   When the U.S. dollar appreciates, it is able to purchase more units of a foreign currency.

2. **CORRECT ANSWER: C**

   The establishment of free trade between nations allows goods and services to be bought and sold without added costs or restrictions. As a result, nations can gain from trade if they specialize in production in which they have a comparative advantage.

   INCORRECT ANSWER

   Free trade is the removal of trade restrictions that emcumber the flow of goods and services between economies. Without these restrictions, economies can maximize their gains from trade.

3. **CORRECT ANSWER: C**

   A tariff is a tax on goods imported from other nations. Tariffs make imports more expensive for domestic consumers. American producers facing foreign competition benefit from tariffs.

   INCORRECT ANSWER

   A tariff is a tax on goods imported from other nations.

4. **CORRECT ANSWER: E**

   A depreciation of the U.S. dollar makes American goods relatively cheaper to foreign consumers. Any agent conducting a transaction that requires the purchase of U.S. dollars will benefit.

5. **CORRECT ANSWER: D**

A tariff is a tax on imported goods. Generally, tariffs cause an increase in the price of imported goods, which benefits domestic producers of goods that face foreign competition. However, enacting tariffs discourages the free exchange of goods among economies. Tariffs stand as an obstacle to experiencing gains through trade.

INCORRECT ANSWER

When nations engage in free trade, they can consume more efficiently.

6. **CORRECT ANSWER: B**

When the government's budget deficit increases, it increases its demand for loanable funds, resulting in an increase in the real interest rate. Foreign investors will increase their demand for the domestic currency, causing it to appreciate. As a result, net exports will decrease.

INCORRECT ANSWER

When the government's budget deficit increases, it increases its demand for loanable funds, resulting in an increase in the real interest rate. How will the resulting change in capital flows affect the exchange rate and net exports?

7. **CORRECT ANSWER: D**

A sale of bonds by the Fed is a contractionary monetary policy that will decrease the inflation rate. As prices decline in the United States, its exports will increase as foreign consumers take advantage of lower prices. Their increasing demand for U.S. goods will cause an appreciation of the U.S. dollar.

INCORRECT ANSWER

A sale of bonds by the Fed is a contractionary monetary policy that will decrease the inflation rate. As prices in the U.S. decline, how will exports and the exchange rate be affected?

Made in the USA
Coppell, TX
06 November 2024

39760112R00174